Government on Fire

Government on Fire

The History and Archaeology
of Upper Canada's First Parliament Buildings

Frank A. Dieterman and Ronald F. Williamson

eastendbooks
Toronto 2001

Design and Production by David Robertson
Printed in Canada by Métrolitho

Cover illustration: The first Parliament buildings rebuilt after the fire of 1813, as depicted by Robert Irvine in a detail from the painting *View of York*, c. 1816. Oil on canvas, 67.6 x 90.5 cm. Art Gallery of Ontario, Toronto. Gift of the descendants of the late Mrs. Stephen Heward, a daughter of the Hon. George Crookshank and cousin of the artist who painted the picture, 1953. *(AGO 52/32)*.

Unless otherwise indicated, the source for all illustrations is Archaeological Services Inc.

National Library of Canada Cataloguing in Publication Data

Dieterman, Frank A., 1961–
    Government on fire: the history and archaeology of Upper Canada's first parliament buildings

Includes index.
ISBN 1-896973-26-4

    1. Parliament buildings (Toronto, Ont.)—History.
2. Toronto (Ont.)—Antiquities. I. Williamson, R.F. (Ronald F.) II. Title.

FC3097.39.D43 2001   971.3'541   C2001-902783-4
F1059.5.T6847D43 2001

eastendbooks is an imprint of Venture Press
45 Fernwood Park Avenue
Toronto, Canada M4E 3E9
(416) 691-6816 (telephone)
(416) 691-2414 (fax)
www.eastendbooks.com

Project Personnel

Project Director	Dr. Ronald F. Williamson
Field Archaeologists	Mr. Andrew Clish
	Dr. Frank A. Dieterman
	Ms. Beverly Garner
	Ms. Irena Miklavcic
	Ms. Debbie Steiss
Artifact Processing	Ms. Liz Truchanowicz
Research Contributors	Mr. Chris Andreae, Historica Research Ltd.
	Dr. Carl Benn, Culture Division, City of Toronto
	Mr. Rollo Myers
	Mr. Stephen Otto
	Dr. Peter von Bitter, Royal Ontario Museum
Graphics	Mr. Andrew Clish
	Dr. Frank A. Dieterman
	Ms. Beverly Garner
	Ms. Irena Miklavcic
Faunal Analysis	Mr. Stephen Cox Thomas, Bioarchaeological Research
Palaeobotanical Analysis	Dr. Stephen G. Monckton, Bioarchaeological Research

Acknowledgements

The investigation of the Parliament site was conducted on behalf of the Heritage Preservation Services of the City of Toronto's Culture Division, who co-ordinated the access and shared funding arrangements with the landowners, Budget Car Rentals Toronto Limited and Auto World Imports.

The completion of the project would not have been possible without the sincere commitment of the Culture Division to the conservation of significant archaeological features within the City of Toronto. In particular, we acknowledge the interest and support of Sean Fraser, formerly a preservation officer with Heritage Preservation Services. His assistance and guidance throughout both the fieldwork and report preparation phases were invaluable. We also acknowledge the interest and assistance of Lance Alexander, senior planner, Community Planning, Urban Development Services.

The impetus for undertaking the archaeological assessment of the Parliament site, however, lies with the heritage advocacy group The Citizens for the Old Town. By contending that an archaeological assessment of the site should be conducted regardless of past impacts, Rollo Myers, Parliament site co-ordinator with The Citizens for the Old Town, can be credited with this astounding and significant historical discovery. Without Mr. Myers' efforts and persistence, it is unlikely that the project would have been undertaken and this important site conserved.

We also acknowledge the technical assistance and expert opinions provided by Chris Andreae (Historica Research Limited), Carl Benn (Culture Division, City of Toronto), Peter Carruthers, Neal Ferris, and Malcolm Horne (Ontario Ministry of Tourism, Culture, and Recreation), David Dennis (formerly with Gooderham and Worts), Dena Doroszenko (Ontario Heritage Foundation), Caroline Phillips (Parks Canada), David Spittal (Fort York), Paul Litt (Ontario Heritage Foundation), Michael McClelland (E.R.A. Architect Inc.), Stephen Otto, and Peter von Bitter (Royal Ontario Museum).

Special thanks must go, however, to Chris Andreae, Carl Benn, Dena Doroszenko, Stephen Otto, and David Spittal. These individuals contributed enormously to our research and writing. While Dr. Benn, Ms. Doroszenko, and Mr. Spittal provided us with copies of relevant archival documents and archaeological literature, as well as information regarding comparable archaeological features, Stephen Otto generously provided access to his collection of primary research material relating to the occupational history of the property. Dr. Benn and Mr. Otto also provided editorial assistance with various sections of the report. Mr. Otto also provided historical expertise on an on-going basis throughout the project. Mr. Andreae's research on the Consumers' Gas use of the property, which he authored in our original technical report, was heavily drawn upon for this volume. The guidance and assistance of these experts were essential to the successful completion of this project.

There was also significant interest in the site from various levels of government. We thank all of those who visited the Parliament site as representatives of the public and /or their offices: Lieutenant Governor Hilary Weston, Member of Parliament Bill Graham, Members of Provincial Parliament George Smitherman and Rosario Marchese, City Councillors Pam McConnell and Kyle Rae, and Phillip Hoffman, Consul for Public Affairs, U.S. Embassy.

This project would not have been possible without the remarkable efforts of the ASI staff members, listed on page v, who completed the fieldwork, laboratory processing, data analyses, graphics, and report preparation. Additional thanks are also due to Irena Miklavcic, David Robertson, Deborah Steiss, and Richard Stromberg for their editorial assistance. Ms. Miklavcic's and Mr. Robertson's dedication and commitment were instrumental in the project reaching fruition. Jeanne MacDonald, Nadine Stoikoff, and Randall White, of eastendbooks, provided great assistance in the production of this volume.

Finally, a steady stream of people made their way to the site over the two-week period that the excavation was open. To all the citizens of Toronto who stopped by on their way to and from work, or made special trips to visit the site, we are grateful for your support and interest.

Frank A. Dieterman
Ronald F. Williamson
Toronto, 2001

Table of Contents

Table of Contents

Figures

Colour Plates
Located following pages 22 and 54

Abbreviations for Commonly Cited Sources of Illustrations

1

INTRODUCTION

This book is an account of the discovery of the archaeological remains of the
first Parliament buildings of Upper Canada. While most people assumed that
it would be unlikely that any deposits associated with the parliamentary
complex would have survived in an urban environment in which there had
been substantial institutional and industrial development, The Citizens for
the Old Town, a local heritage advocacy group, persisted. As a result of their
commitment over the years, the archaeological consulting firm of
Archaeological Services Inc. (ASI), based in Toronto, was contracted by the
Culture Division, Economic Development, Culture and Tourism
Department, City of Toronto, to conduct an archaeological assessment in
search of any surviving remains of the parliamentary complex. The search was
focussed on portions of the lands bounded by Berkeley Street to the west,
Front Street to the north, Parliament Street to the east, and the original shore
of Lake Ontario to the south. Historians have long known that this site was
the location of the first and second Parliament buildings of Upper Canada,
built in 1797 and 1820, respectively. Indeed, the City of Toronto designated
the properties under the Ontario Heritage Act in 1997. What is most amaz-
ing, however, is that the buried remains of the Parliament buildings, while
undoubtedly affected by the industrial development of the property, were not
completely destroyed. On that small block of land flanked to the east and
west by soaring Victorian façades, traces of Upper Canada's Parliament buildings' past remained.

The property has had many uses over the years. Ruins of the Parliament
buildings were demolished prior to erecting new structures and it was
thought that the foundations for later buildings would have damaged any
remaining buried remnants. Therefore, a series of map overlays was used to
determine areas with the least disturbance, and thus the highest potential for
finding portions of the Parliament buildings. In one of the test trenches excavated over a two-week period in the fall of 2000, both structural remains and
artifacts dating to the parliamentary period were discovered.

While a detailed report on the excavations and subsequent analyses (ASI 2001) that was prepared for the City of Toronto is available, this present volume provides a more general summary of the history and archaeology of the site. The following two chapters present summaries of the historical and cartographic research conducted for the project, while Chapter 4 provides an account of the archaeological features and recovered artifacts. Indeed, the architectural remains and artifacts, which were recovered from the site, have been subjected to intense analysis. The analyses were conducted by a number of specialists, including architectural historians who examined the structure of the footings and the materials used to make them; geologists who analyzed the stone in the footings; a palaeo-botanist who examined the pollen record below the floor of the building and the wood from which the floorboards were fashioned; an archaeo-zoologist who analyzed the recovered animal bones; and historic archaeologists who examined the recovered artifact assemblage.

Each of these analyses reached independent conclusions which together provide compelling evidence for the association of these deposits with Upper Canada's first Parliament buildings. The final chapter summarizes this collective evidence and provides the reader with a rare glimpse into how the archaeological and archival records combined to confirm the survival of a piece of our past.

Moreover, the soil layers in the walls of the excavation suggest that more of this buried feature remains intact under the paved surface. Given the significance of the site to the history of Toronto, Ontario, and Canada, it now falls on all of us to advocate for the long term conservation and interpretation of this important place.

2

BEFORE THE CARWASH

The lands at Front and Parliament streets contain a car wash, rental car agency, parking lot, and empty buildings from a former automotive centre. The history of the site, however, is far more complex and impressive than its current, rather unassuming, appearance suggests.

In 1793, Lieutenant Governor John Graves Simcoe (Figure 2.1) founded the Town of York, now known as Toronto. The town site proper extended from Lake Ontario to modern Queen Street (then known as Lot Street). Lands to the west and east of the town site were reserved for the Crown: the "Garrison Reserve" lay to the west of modern Peter Street, while the area between modern Berkeley Street and the Don River was called "The Park." The first Parliament site was in The Park.

The first Parliament buildings of Upper Canada stood from 1797 to 1813, when they were burned by American forces during the War of 1812. They consisted of two one-and-one-half-storey, brick structures (see cover) with two smaller frame buildings to the east. In 1820, a new seat of government was built on the same site. The design reconstructed the original buildings as wings and filled the space between with a centre block. It only stood until 1824, when it also burned — this time, accidentally.

In 1837–1840, the Home District Gaol (the old spelling of jail, but pronounced the same) was built on the site. The limestone gaol featured a five-storey central tower and two three-storey radial wings. It was used only from 1840 to 1864.

In 1887, the Consumers' Gas Company, which occupied several blocks in the Front and Parliament area, demolished the gaol. In its place, it erected an office building that faced Front Street and was flanked by two retort buildings, extending approximately 80 metres south from Front Street, along Berkeley and Parliament streets. A single, sunken rail spur extended from the space between the southerly reaches of the retort buildings, southwestward to the rail corridor along the lakeshore. Consumers' Gas sold the site in the 1960s, at which time it was redeveloped to its current configuration.

3

Figure 2.1. John Graves Simcoe (1752–1806), the first Lieutenant Governor of Upper Canada. *(TL 1516)*

Upper Canada's First Parliament Buildings, 1797–1818

A New Capital, 1793–1797

Lieutenant Governor John Graves Simcoe first visited the future site of Toronto in May 1793, but the potential of the natural harbour of Toronto Bay was already well known. Alexander Aitkin produced the first survey of Toronto Harbour in 1788 (Figure 2.2) and Captain Gother Mann's plan of the same year proposed a permanent European settlement on Toronto Bay (Firth 1962:21).

Having inspected Toronto Bay himself, Simcoe agreed that the defensible harbour would be "indispensible for the protection of the Province" (Firth 1962:5), and on 30 July 1793, he returned with his wife and the Queens Rangers. He set out to fortify the harbour and to establish a settlement. On 26 August 1793, he named the new town "York" to honour the Duke of York (Firth 1962:7).

Figure 2.2. Detail from Alexander Aitkin, *A Plan of the Harbour of Toronto with a proposed Town and Settlement,* 1788, showing the reserved land east of the planned town. *(NAC NMC-0022816)*

Simcoe's actions and historical documents make it clear that his first priority was to strengthen the British military's position in Upper Canada. In 1794, Simcoe moved the capital from Newark (Niagara-on-the-Lake) to York as a temporary measure to place it in a more secure location. He did so because the war in the Ohio country between the native peoples and the United States threatened to spread into Canada, especially with the collateral problems arising out of the Anglo-French war that had started in 1793. In 1796, the decision was then made to keep the capital in York because the Jay's Treaty of 1794, which eased Anglo-American tensions, had, as one of its provisions, the transfer of Fort Niagara from British to American control (in return for some American concessions). Accordingly, officials thought that the capital could not be located at a site within range of an American fort (Benn 1993).

Simcoe had not intended York to be the seat of government, preferring instead a site on the Thames River to be named London. Home Secretary Henry Dundas, however, also concerned with the military defence of Upper Canada, settled the matter in a dispatch from Whitehall on 16 March 1794:

> I also agree with you that the place upon the River Thames which You have marked as the Scite for London, is well situated & judiciously chosen for the future Capital, but as the defence of the Colony is the first object, if that defence should be Maritime, it

follows that the Settlement of York is the most important for the present, not as the future Capital, but as the Chief place of strength & security for the Naval force of the Province (Firth 1962:27).

Peter Russell (Figure 2.3) was one of the first to support York as an "establishment," noting on 16 September 1793 that he was "charmed with the Situation of the proposed City of York in the Bay of Toronto" (Firth 1962:17). Russell then proclaimed the advantages of the town site as both wholly out of the way and perfectly defensible against any American and native incursions (Firth 1962:20). In the autumn of 1793, Simcoe informed the officials at Newark that York was to be the temporary seat of government for Upper Canada. However, in a prescient statement, Russell observed concurrently, "… it is impossible to say how soon the Town & Country round [York] may be sufficiently inhabited to warrant the removal of the public offices thither …" (Firth 1962:21). Indeed, when Simcoe left Upper Canada in the summer of 1796, not one of the senior civilian officials had arrived in York.

The early development of Simcoe's Town of York was shaped by a 1793 plan by Alexander Aitkin (Figure 2.4). The town was situated between Lake Ontario and Lot Street (modern Queen Street). The Aitkin plan also established

Figure 2.3. Peter Russell (1733–1808), Administrator of Upper Canada from 1796 to 1799. *(OA S/2014)*

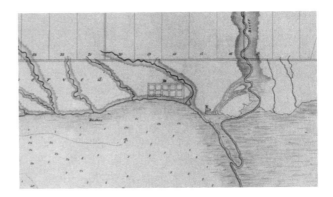

Figure 2.4. Detail from Alexander Aitkin, *Plan of York Harbour*, 1793, showing the planned Town of York. *(NAC NMC-0021768)*

hundred-acre "park lots" between Lot and Bloor streets, which were to be granted to officials in compensation for leaving the comforts of Newark for the wilderness of York (Firth 1962:xxxvi). Most importantly for the Parliament site, Aitkin's earlier plan was the first to show land set aside for the Crown including The Park and Garrison Reserve.

The proposal to build Parliament buildings at York was clearly stated by the Lieutenant Governor in a letter to the Duke of Portland, dated 27 February 1796:

> I have given information to the Civil officers of Government that
> *York*, for the present, is to become the Seat of Government, & in
> consequence, I am preparing to erect such Buildings as may be
> necessary for the future meeting of the Legislature, the plan I have
> adopted is, to consider a future Government House, as a Center,
> & to construct the *Wings* as temporary Offices for the legislature.
> Proposing that so soon as the Province has sufficient Funds to
> erect its own Public Buildings, that They may be removed else-
> where (Firth 1962:24).

The following day, E.B. Littlehales, Simcoe's military secretary in Upper Canada, penned a circular ordering the officials Peter Russell, William Jarvis, D.W. Smith, and Dr. David Burns to move their offices to York:

> I have the honour to signify to you His Excellency, the Lieut.
> Governor's directions, that immediately upon the conclusion of
> the ensuing meeting of the Provincial Parliament, you will be
> pleased to remove your office to York, the present Seat of this
> Government (Firth 1962:25).

As noted, the order was unpopular and officials were reluctant to move. Even Peter Russell, who had extolled the virtues of York, delayed his move and was forced to respond to Simcoe on 25 June 1796: "It has excited in me no small Pain to observe that this is the third Mandate I have received by your Excellencys Orders, on this Subject; because it seems to imply a suspected unwillingness on my Part to execute your Excellencys Commands ..." (Firth 1962:31). Russell, however, quickly made amends by acting decisively and wisely on matters affecting the Town of York between 1796 and 1799, when he was the administrator of the province during Simcoe's absence on home leave. Simcoe left Upper Canada in 1796 without seeing York come into its own as a successful capital and commercial centre. He also never saw his Parliament buildings completed.

Construction of the First Parliament Buildings, 1795–1797

The first documented communication between Lieutenant Governor Simcoe and Commissary John McGill, the government official responsible for public buildings, regarding the construction of the Parliament buildings at York was dated 1 December 1795 and was very detailed:

> You are hereby required and directed to employ a party of the Queen's Rangers in Opening a Road, and making Bridges, between the Garrison and Town of York — You are also directed to employ a party of the said Queens Rangers in cutting wood for Burning Bricks, clearing the Ground of Trees and Roots whereon the Government House is to be built at York, and in Turning up Clay for Bricks — You are likewise to engage a sufficient number of Men to Mould and Burn a quantity of Bricks to Build two wings for the Government House, forty feet long, each as soon as the season will permit — You are also to engage Bricklayers, Masons, Carpenters, & Laborers and to pay the same, as well as to issue & provide from Time to Time such Stores and Materials as may be required for the said Service, and for two Frame houses, each thirty feet long, adjoining to the two wings for Committee Rooms to the two Houses during the sitting of the Legislature — and for so doing this shall be your warrant and Authority (Canada Papers, 1793-1834).

Further references to the frame houses are rare, but they were depicted on a number of plans (e.g., Figures 2.5 and 2.6). A 1799 reference noted that the houses were to be moved to the front and used as guard houses for the proposed Lieutenant Governor's house (Firth 1962:52–53).

Simcoe wrote again to McGill, on 17 March 1796, regarding the hauling of materials for the buildings:

> You are hereby required and directed to contract for a quantity of Rails sufficient to enclose a part of the Lands attached to the Government Houses at York, for the purposes of keeping the Horses and Oxen during the time their services may be required

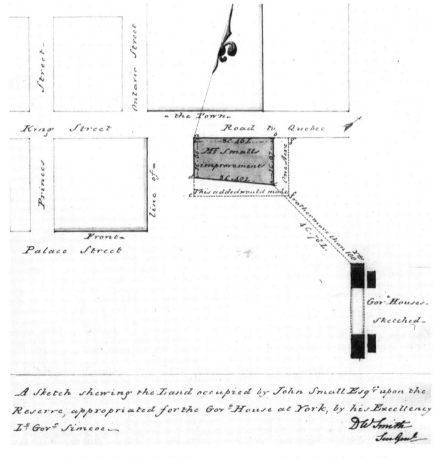

Figure 2.5. D.W. Smith, *Mr. Small's Improvements* … 1805, showing John Small's property and the relationship with the first Parliament buildings. *(TL DW Smith Papers B9-311)*

in Hauling Wood, Stone, Brick, Sand and Lime for the Public
Buildings ... (Canada Papers, 1793–1834).

In July of 1794, the *Upper Canada Gazette*, the first paper to be published
in the new province, printed an advertisement, which read: "Wanted, carpenters for the public buildings to be erected at York. Applications to be
made to John McGill Esq. at York or to Mr. Allan McNab at Navy Hall
(Newark)."

Plans for the Parliament buildings were drawn by William Graham, a
master carpenter who was also appointed to supervise the construction. The
construction work was undertaken by Ephraim Payson, the Government
bricklayer, and a crew working under David Thomson, a Scottish stonema-
son who arrived in Canada in June 1796 and was later the first settler in the
Township of Scarborough (Arthur 1986:27–28, Richardson and Otto 1993).
Throughout the fall, the *Upper Canada Gazette* contained a weekly advertisement for "a few good house carpenters for the public buildings at York to
whom good encouragement will be given" (Arthur 1979, Dale 1993:9, 72).

Peter Russell recorded the progress of the work in a letter to Governor-in-
Chief Robert Prescott, dated 28 February 1797:

> A Dwelling House for the Governor and Buildings to receive the
> two Houses of Legislature had been ordered by Lieut. Governor
> Simcoe before his Departure, and are now erecting under the
> directions of Mr. Commissary McGill. These will of course require
> the Occasional aid of Troops, which in my humble opinion are
> indispensible also for giving Energy, Respectability and Protection
> to the Civil Governt (Firth 1962:39).

Graham's original plan also called for a central section (no copy of his plan
survives). It quickly became apparent, however, that the cost of the central
section would be prohibitive. The size of the two wings was modified and a
new plan for joining them was proposed by Robert Pilkington, as detailed in
a letter dated 15 March 1797 from Russell to McGill:

> Since my last I have had an Opportunity of speaking with Mr.
> Pilkington, and very much approve of the Alterations he proposes
> for the Government House — By these the two Wings will be 40
> by 24 feet and joined to the Body of the House by something like
> a Colonade — But it will be necessary to advance the House as

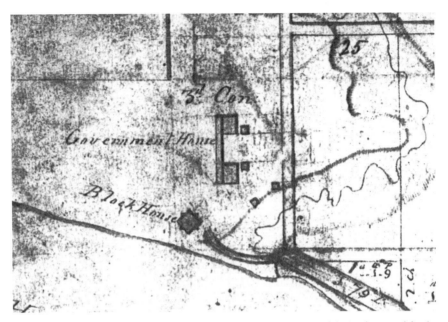

Figure 2.6. Detail from Samuel Wilmot, *A Plan Showing the Survey of the land Reserved for the Government Buildings ...* 1810, showing Parliament buildings, frame houses, and town block-house. *(OSR Microfiche 390 File H-26)*

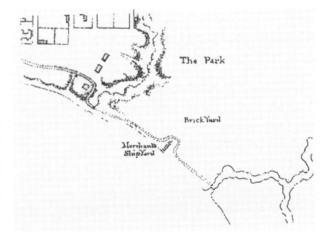

Figure 2.7. Detail from George Williams, *A Sketch of the Ground ... at York,* 1813, showing the Parliament build-ings and town block-house. *(NAC NMC-22819)*

well as them Several Paces, and they will of course occupy a larger space in front than Mr. Grahams plan.

In the mean time your three Carpenters may be employed in plan-ing the flooring & trying up the stuff for Windows and Doors … . It is not my intention to Attempt more at present than the two Wings, as before they are finished I may expect to receive final Instructions from home, which will determine me respecting the propriety of entering into so large an Expence as the Mansion will assuredly prove. — But these two wings by being joined by a tem-porary covered way to the two Buildings in the rear, — may be of great use for the present, — as Houses for the meeting of the Legislature, holding Councils[,] giving entertainments in, and back appartments for occasional lodgings (Firth 1962:39–40).

David Thomson's account book for 1797 recorded details regarding con-struction activities, the names of employees, and the pace of work. For exam-ple, the task of bricking and plastering the Government Houses was com-pleted over a two-and-one-half-month period by Ephriam Payson and a crew consisting of David Thomson, his brother Andrew, and nephew John, as well as Andrew Johnstone and James Elliot (Richardson and Otto 1993). An entry in the journal of David Thomson states: "July 26th Begun to wall the Government Brick houses. 53,500 brick at £17/6 per thousand" (Thomson 1797). An undated entry notes that "plastering the two Government Rooms" was completed by the three Thomsons over a period of fourteen days (Thomson 1797).

Information on costs has also survived. A receipt for £51/0/3 was issued on 12 October 1797 to Andrew and David Thomson, "For Building One wing to the intended Government House at York, 53,500 Bricks at £17/6 [per thousand] for Mason work & Laborers between the 25th July & 10th October 1797 inclusive [and] for laying 84 feet of Arches at 1/ per foot" (Canada Papers, 1793–1834).

It only took two and a half months to erect and plaster one wing, which was apparently the south one. The north wing was not completed until much later, as is evident in John McGill's lament to Peter Russell on November 5, 1797:

I am sorry, that I have no power or authority over the Carpenters employed at work on the Government House, to order them upon any other service, unless they will agree to do it from choice … .

12

> But I must beg at the same time to state, that it is highly expedient and necessary that the wing of the Government House should be enclosed and secured against damage by Frost, without the least possible delay, in order to preserve the Brickwork from utter destruction, after the great expence which has been already incurred & exertions made to have the House erected and enclosed before the winter sett in, and after having pressed and sollicited Major Shank for Masons and Labourers to bring the Building to a finish — I should humbly conceive myself not justificable to the Public, did I not persevere and by every means in my power endeavor to secure the Building in such a manner as to preserve the Brickwork from tumbling down. By the injury which if left in its present State, it would assuredly receive during the Winter (Firth 1962:44–45).

Apparently, the situation was quickly rectified. A letter from Russell to Simcoe, dated 9 December 1797, described the now completed Parliament buildings:

> The Two wings to the Government House are raised with Brick & completely covered in. The South One, being in the greatest forwardness I have directed to be fited up for a temporary Court House for the Kings Bench in the ensuing Term, and I hope they may both be in a condition to receive the Two Houses of Parliament in June next, I have not yet given directions for proceeding with the remainder of your Excellency's plan for the Government House, being alarmed at the magnitude of the expence which Captain Graham estimates at (£10,000) I shall however order a large Kiln of Bricks to be prepared in the Spring and burnt (as they will readily sell for what they cost if Government does not want them) and Boards & Scantling may be cut and seasoned upon the same principle (Firth 1962:46).

While Russell described the buildings in words in 1797, they were first depicted graphically in an 1805 survey sketch by D.W. Smith (Figure 2.5). Numerous other plans, surveys, and paintings produced between 1803 and 1813 (Plate 1, Figures 2.6 and 2.7) displayed a variety of images and orientations for the Parliament buildings.

In summary, the first Parliament buildings of Upper Canada consisted of two brick structures measuring 40 feet by 24 feet and situated 75 feet apart. The Legislative Council sat in the southern building and the House of

Assembly in the northern building. The buildings were likely one and a half storeys in height, each with a small viewing gallery to which access was by a staircase. Immediately east of the brick buildings were two 30-foot-long frame dwellings used for committee rooms. The widths of these two frame buildings are unknown and cannot be inferred since they are clearly depicted only on the Smith (Figure 2.5) and Wilmot (Figure 2.6) plans, but with different configurations.

Maintenance, 1797–1813

The first Parliament to meet in the buildings was convened by the Honourable Peter Russell, President of the Legislative Council, in June 1797, and sat for eight weeks (Arthur 1979:33). The brick Parliament buildings gave York an aura of permanence and were a source of pride. East of Jarvis Street, Front Street was named Palace Street to celebrate the "Palaces of Government." On 5 June 1798, it was recorded that the parliamentary members "acknowledge our obligations … for providing so suitable a House for our temporary reception" (Journal of the Commons House of Assembly 1798:132).

Nevertheless, the shortcomings of York's public buildings emerged quickly. In a lengthy communication from Lieutenant Governor Peter Hunter to Lord Hobart, Secretary for War and the Colonies, dated 10 April 1804, he complained that £400 yearly set aside as a building fund for new Parliament buildings was far from sufficient. This allowance had been instituted by an act of the Legislature in February 1804, but by 1808 was repealed due to its inadequacy (Dale 1993:11). Hunter requested "liberal aid" similar to that which Lower Canada had received:

> I have the honour to transmit to your Lordship an Address to His Majesty by the two Houses of Legislature in this Province.
> Your Lordship will perceive, that the Object which the prayer of this Address has in View, is an Aid from the United Empire, to enable the Province to erect at the Seat of Government proper Buildings for the preservation of the public Records, the Assembling of the Legislative Council and House of Assembly, and for Courts of Justice, and the transacting the other public Business (Firth 1962:55).

The request was rejected.

William Smith submitted a proposal on 21 November 1805 for the first recorded alteration to the first Parliament buildings. Smith was asked to build a covered walkway between the two brick buildings:

> The Platform is to be 75 feet long, 12 feet 6 inches wide, to be covered with 1/2 inch plank, the posts to be 8 feet high above the top of the Platform and to be covered with 3/4 inch boards on the east side, the frame to be done according to plan, the roof to be boarded with inch boards (Upper Canada Sundries 1805).

Subsequently approved and constructed "According to Contract," Smith submitted a bill for £18 on 7 January 1806 (Papers of Executive Council of Upper Canada 1806).

A year later, the Speaker, Alex McDonnell, wrote on 22 November 1806 to Major Halton (Secretary to Lieutenant Governor Francis Gore) that the House of Assembly was in much need of repair. He observed that the building was not fit for a reception of the House. On 27 November 1806, McDonnell submitted an estimate prepared by John McBeath of £27/15/0 for repairs consisting of "putting in Sleepers and laying a floor in the House of Assembly and ditto in the Portico, Taking down and putting up the Gallery, Taking down and putting up the columns" (Upper Canada Sundries 1806). The Lieutenant Governor approved the repairs on 18 January 1808, and McBeath submitted an invoice for the completed work in April 1808 (Papers of Executive Council of Upper Canada 1808).

Ancillary Uses of the First Parliament Buildings, 1797–1813

The Parliament buildings at York were used for many government and public functions (Dale 1993:9) beyond the sitting of the legislature, which was typically for only two months of the year. This multifaceted use was described in Hunter's letter of 1804 to Hobart noted previously:

> As to the Building at present appropriated to the meeting of the two houses of Legislature, and for the Court of Appeal, the Court of King's Bench, the District Court and the Quarter Sessions, it only consists of two Rooms, erected about 8 or 9 years ago, as a small part of what was at that time intended for a Government house.

15

> The Building is also obliged to make use of for many other pub-
> lic Purposes, among the Rest as a Church … . Neither is it calcu-
> lated for any of these Uses, and it has been with the greatest diffi-
> culty and attended with every possible Inconvenience that the
> public Business has been hitherto carried on … (Firth 1962:55).

The most notable occupant was the Anglican Church. While the congregation had met in various public buildings, including the town gaol, they met
most frequently in the Parliament buildings between 1797 and 1807. A subscription to build a church was begun in 1803, although it was not completed until 1807 (Benn 1998:7). It would appear that the congregation was sufficiently satisfied with the Parliament buildings that no extraordinary efforts
were made to expedite construction of a church (Benn 1998:8).

Indeed, the population was apparently not sufficiently pious to attend
services, for in 1804, Rev. G.O. Stuart stated that he had made some progress
in increasing attendance, although the labouring class consisted "almost
wholly of disbanded soldiers, whose manner of life has been ill calculated
either to improve or preserve their morals." The élite were no better, for "by
his reckoning, prominent parishioners included at least six men who kept
mistresses and not a gentlemen save Mr. Small honestly 'profess our religion'"
(Benn 1998:10). It is not surprising, therefore, that the Parliament buildings
served as the church at York for a full decade.

The history of Upper Canada's first Parliament buildings extends beyond
the physical structures. A duel was fought on the grounds of the Parliament
buildings, in 1800, between Major John Small, Clerk of the Executive
Council, and Attorney General John White, as "Small challenged White
when the Attorney General refused to withdraw slanderous comments about
the virtue of Major Small's wife" (Dale 1993:9). White was shot in the hip
and later died as a result of this injury. Small was arrested and charged with
murder but was acquitted, as was the custom of the time for duels over matters of honour.

The Town Blockhouse, 1799–1813

The Parliament site also had a military presence. Peter Russell is usually
remembered for his provincial administration, but he also added to Simcoe's
fortifications. The town blockhouse was built in 1799. Its primary role was

to deter aboriginal incursions into the Town of York and to serve as the rallying point of the York Militia (Benn 1993:34–39). In a letter to Lieutenant Governor Peter Hunter, dated 20 August 1799, Russell wrote that he was constructing "a defensible Guard House intended … to cover such Troops as might be judged necessary for the Protection of the Town" (Firth 1962:49). He added that the Guard House was not yet complete.

A sketch by William Leney (Plate 2), dated November 1812, showed the town blockhouse on a bluff less than ten metres from the Lake Ontario shore. Its location relative to the first Parliament buildings can be seen on the 1810 Wilmot Survey (Figure 2.6).

William Graham, the carpenter who designed the Parliament buildings, also designed the blockhouse. It was a two-storey log structure, measuring 28 feet square at the base. The square upper storey peaked at 21 feet and was offset 45 degrees to provide clear lines of sight in all directions, and was to include seven windows (three lower and four upper) and a single doorway.

Graham's estimate specified the materials and costs for transporting the materials to the site. He requested thousands of feet of squared pine, oak, and unspecified timbers; seven window frames; three window shutters; one door and frame; flooring; hardware; eight barrels of lime; 5,750 two-foot shingles; 14,000 nails; and an additional 12,000 six-penny nails. Russell approved the design and ordered contracts for close to £200 to be entered into on 26 February 1799 (Papers of Executive Council of Upper Canada 1799).

The town blockhouse was equipped with a kitchen so that it could also be used as a barracks for up to 48 men (Benn 1995:26). In November 1801, Æneas Shaw, Lieutenant of York County, wrote to Lord Dorchester's military secretary that "The Kitchens at the Block House in Town have been long finished, but I am sorry to say that I have not yet been able to … send a Party to occupy them … but in a few days I shall be able to send some men there although not quite the number directed" (Firth 1962:71).

The American invasion in 1813 proved that Russell had anticipated correctly the need for better defences. The town blockhouse, however, was not needed. Indeed, on the 1816 Nicolls plan it is noted that, "the Battery had all guns and were made use of on the 27th April [l813], except the one at the marsh [a reference to the low-lying marshes east of the Parliament site]" (Nicolls 1816). The town blockhouse was, nevertheless, burned by the Americans and never rebuilt.

Burning of the First Parliament Buildings, 1813

On 27 April 1813, the U.S. Army and Navy mounted an attack on York dispatching a force of 2,650 men on 14 ships and schooners, armed with 85 cannon. The defending force of 750 British, Canadians, Mississaugas, and Ojibways had 12 cannon. The Americans stormed ashore west of Fort York under the cover of the naval guns. The defenders put up a strong fight, but fell back to the fort from the landing site in the face of overwhelming odds. The British commander, Major-General Sir Roger Sheaffe, then retreated eastward and blew up the fort's gunpowder magazine. The explosion was devastating; 250 Americans fell dead or wounded from its blast, including their field commander, Brigadier-General Zebulon Pike. Total losses in the six-hour battle were 157 British and 320 Americans. The Mississaugas and Ojibways withdrew into the forest, Sheaffe's professional troops retreated to Kingston, and the local militia surrendered the town. The Americans occupied York for six days. They looted homes, took or destroyed supplies, and burned various public facilities, including Government House at Fort York and the Parliament buildings and neighbouring blockhouse. On 1 May the Americans boarded their ships. They then rode at anchor in the harbour to wait out a storm, sailing from York on 8 May (Benn 1993:50–62).

First-hand accounts and reports of the day best describe events of the invasion. On 19 March 1814, John Beikie, a volunteer with the Grenadier Company of the 8th Regiment, wrote:

> The moment they [the Yankees] got in they began to plunder and burn the public Buildings, which they continued for four days when they went on Board where they rode at Anchor from the 1st to the 8th of May inclusive. The public Buildings burnt on this occasion were — The Governt. House, the Block House at the Garrison ... the Brick Buildings at the East end of the Town and Mr. Russell's Block House (Firth 1962:329).

In the 17 August 1813 issue of the *Kingston Gazette,* a letter, signed "Falkland," was printed:

> They [the Americans at York], it is true, entered into a formal stipulation not only that private property should be respected, but that papers belonging to the Civil Departments of the Government should not be removed or destroyed. Yet the first

object they selected for depredation was the Printing Office. They broke and otherwise destroyed the Press; carried off or rendered useless the Types; and burned a large number of Copies of the Provincial Statutes that had been recently printed for general distribution. They then pillaged the Public Subscription Library kept at Elmsley House, carried away a great part of the Books, and did a great injury to the house itself. And, to crown all, before they re-embarked they set fire to the two houses erected for the accomodation of our Provincial Legislature and Courts of Justice, which … were neat and substantial buildings, and had been erected and fitted up at an expense of several thousand pounds. These with the Offices containing all the Journals, a large collection of Books and other appendages connected with such an establishment, were all consumed by the flames; and the bare walls alone remain, a monument of the Gothic ferocity and worse than Punic faith of our enemies.

The invasion of York resulted in a severe loss of public property, including the complete destruction of the Parliament buildings and the town blockhouse. Among the items taken from the Parliament buildings were a carved lion and the Assembly's ceremonial mace (the symbol of the Assembly's power). President Roosevelt returned the mace to the provincial government in 1934.

There remains some debate about who actually burned the Parliament buildings (West 1967:85). General Dearborn vigorously denied ordering their destruction and the burning might have been "the unauthorized work of American sailors" (Hitsman 1965:127). Regardless, the action spurred a now commonly held belief that the mid-August 1814 British raid on Washington was to avenge the York actions; the presidential mansion was burned in retaliation for the destruction of the Government House, while the Congress was burned in retaliation for the Parliament buildings (Stacey 1963).

The 1814 session of the Parliament of Upper Canada had to meet in the ballroom of the 1796 Jordan's Hotel, at the corner of King and Parliament. Five subsequent sessions, for the years 1815 to 1820, were held in a private residence called "Holyrood House," at the corner of modern Wellington and York streets (Firth 1962:277). An attempt to purchase the property for the government's continued use as a legislature was made in February 1818, but never carried through (Dale 1993:13).

Reuse of the First Parliament Buildings, 1814–1818

There are two documented uses of the first Parliament buildings after 1813: first as temporary barracks for troops following the destruction of the garrison during the war; and then as temporary housing for newly arrived immigrants to York.

Soon after the 1813 American invasion, and while Fort York was being rebuilt, the first Parliament buildings, whose walls had survived the fire, were hastily repaired as two-storey brick structures for billeting 200–300 British troops. On Williams' 1814 plan of York, the Parliament buildings are marked as "Barracks — 220 men" and the presence of a small cookhouse is noted behind the northeast building in the same location as one of the Parliament frame buildings (Figure 2.8). By late 1815 or early 1816, the military reconstruction of the garrison was completed (Carl Benn pers. comm. 2000). Troops would have been billeted at the rebuilt Parliament buildings for at least part of the period between 1813 and 1815.

After the soldiers left, the reconstructed buildings housed newly arrived immigrants. Thomas Stevenson recounted that when he was five years of age, he and his family arrived at York on 19 May 1817 and were billeted for three days in

> the Upper part of the Upper Canada House which Consisted of one large Room Unfurnished. Some one marked on the floor with chalk the bounds of each family was to occupy … the entrance to this wonderful upper house was by an outside wooden Stairway on the South side of the Building (Firth 1966:302).

This use appears to have continued into 1818. A receipt was issued on 9 January to the "No. 1 Brick Building at the lower end of the Town" for 24 1/2

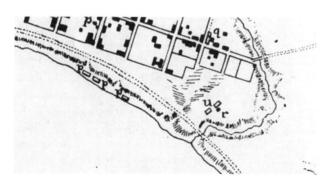

Figure 2.8. Detail from George Williams, *Plan of the Town and Harbour of York*, 1814, showing the barracks (u), formerly the first Parliament buildings, and the cookhouse (r). *(University of Toronto, Map Library, G 3524. T61 1814 MAPL)*

double boards, 226 bottom boards, 74 side boards, and 44 head boards. In addition, "the Cook house attached to the above mentioned Brick Building" was issued four boilers and iron grates, and a small guard bed (Upper Canada Sundries 1818).

The appearance of the rebuilt Parliament buildings was captured in Robert Irvine's circa 1815 oil painting entitled *View of York*. Irvine's movements have been traced from the War of 1812 through 1821. Following Irvine's capture in September 1813 and subsequent release from an American prison by September 1814, he was said to be residing at York. Irvine was employed by the military in the vicinity of York until early 1817, but by April 1820 was resident in Scotland (Otto 1993).

Irvine's painting emphasized the lighthouse at Gibraltar Point (now Hanlan's Point); the two brick Parliament structures were executed as a tiny detail near the right margin (Plate 3). Irvine depicted the west and south faces of two brick buildings of identical design. Upper and lower series of four windows were set along the length of the west walls, and an upper and lower pair of doorways was set in the centre of the south walls. Exterior stairs, originating at the southwest corner of each building, reached the upper doorways. The image is the only one known of the reconstructed first Parliament and it corroborates Stevenson's reminiscences.

Upper Canada's Second Parliament Buildings, 1819–1824

With Parliament meeting in temporary quarters, Francis Gore, Lieutenant Governor from 1808 to 1817, renewed the appeal for British funds for an improved legislature, asking Lord Bathurst, Secretary of State for War and the Colonies,

> for the grant of a Sum of Money, to erect Buildings, for the Accommodation of the Legislative Council, the House of Assembly, and the Courts of Justice, at York in Upper Canada; — The Buildings appropriated for those purposes having been destroyed by the Americans when in possession of that Place … such was the distress for a place to assemble … [that] the Chief Justice would be obliged to hold the sittings in a Tavern (Firth 1966:3).

The British, however, wished to relocate the capital of Upper Canada to Kingston, citing military reasons: York had been attacked three times during the war, while Kingston had not suffered a single American incursion. This idea was not well met by the people of York. Representatives in Britain received indignant letters from Chief Justice Thomas Scott and countersigned by York's most prominent citizens, including John McGill, Samuel Smith, William Jarvis, Thomas Ridout, John Small, William Chewett, D'Arcy Boulton, James Givens, and W.W. Baldwin. The Rev. John Strachan also wrote lengthy oppositions to the proposal. On 12 June 1816, the British government acquiesced and declared that York should be the permanent seat of government (Firth 1966:15).

The defeat of the proposal to move the capital to Kingston gave impetus to the construction of a new Parliament building. In June 1818, acting upon the Legislature's advice, Samuel Smith, Administrator in the absence of Lieutenant Governor Gore, gave instructions to the provincial agent in London to commission two separate sets of plans for government buildings at York, including a building for the accommodation of the two houses of the Legislature. Two architects, Sir John Soane, and his former pupil, David Laing, were invited to prepare plans. In the end Laing was the only one to submit plans, for which he received £157/10/0 (Arthur 1986:57).

Construction, 1818–1820

The estimate of costs for Laing's scheme made the officials at York aware of the enormity of financing new buildings. Faced with a limited budget, they soon abandoned his plans. Instead, the Speakers of the two Houses of Assembly authorized £800, "for temporary accommodation of the two Houses" to supplement £900 already available "by adding to and repairing the brick buildings heretofore used by the provincial Parliament" (Canada Papers, 1793–1834).

A builder contacted in late 1818 or early 1819 to "sketch a project of what would be required" estimated it would cost £3,000 to repair the existing brick ruins "in handsome stile." This included £2,250 to build the "Centre building exclusive of the Wings" and £650 "to put up the walls and complete the Outside of the whole." It was noted that the centre building could not be erected in brick until late 1819 or early 1820, but if a wood structure would suffice it could be finished by the summer of 1819 (Upper Canada State Papers 1819:84).

Plate 1. Detail from Elisabeth Francis Hale, *York on Lake Ontario, Upper Canada,* 1804, watercolour, showing the Parliament buildings and town blockhouse. *(NAC C34334)*

Plate 2. William Leney, *York, on Lake Ontario*, 1812, showing the town blockhouse south of the Parliament buildings. *(TL T10336)*

Plate 7. The brick rubble layer and brown clay, adjacent to the rail spur wall, in Trench 2.

Plate 8. Ronald Williamson (left) and Frank Dieterman examining the blacksmith token.

The decision to build between the brick ruins of the former Parliament was firm, such that, on 18 February 1819, a call for proposals was issued in the *Upper Canada Gazette*. The Managers of Public Buildings Peter Robinson and Grant Powell, reported that the "wishes of the two Houses of Provincial Parliament" were to proceed,

> without delay to close with the lowest proposals for such a building as, together with the old brick building repaired, [these] would in their opinion afford all the accommodation at present actually required for the convenience of the Legislature, at the same time keeping in view the probability of more extensive provision for that purpose being necessary at some future day (Firth 1966:15, see also Dale 1993:14–15).

Proposals were received from Josiah Cushman (Figure 2.9), Jonathan Cassels, and perhaps others. The contract was awarded to Jonathan Cassels, who submitted the lowest bid. He started work immediately. By 4 May 1820, tenders were being called in the *Upper Canada Gazette* for painting the new Parliament buildings. The first session in the new buildings opened in December 1820.

While the second Parliament buildings were "very generally approved" (Firth 1966:308), Scadding (1966:3) described them as more "conspicuous and more capacious," yet "still plain and simply cubical brick block." One early complaint, noted in the *Upper Canada Gazette* of 1821, was that the galleries were neither large enough nor well ventilated.

Accidental Burning of the Second Parliament Buildings, 1824

The second Parliament buildings, like the first, were destroyed by fire. On 30 December 1824, a fire broke out in the north wing, likely due to sparks from an overheated chimney flue. According to the *Upper Canada Gazette,* published that same day, the fire was swift and destructive, burning with "such irresistible fury as to defeat every effort to save that wing, and the main body of the building; — the southern wing was saved by dint of long continued and strenuous exertion, but not without considerable injury being done to it" (Firth 1966:268). Following the fire, Grant Powell, Clerk of the House of Assembly, wrote to George Hillier, private secretary to Lieutenant Governor Maitland:

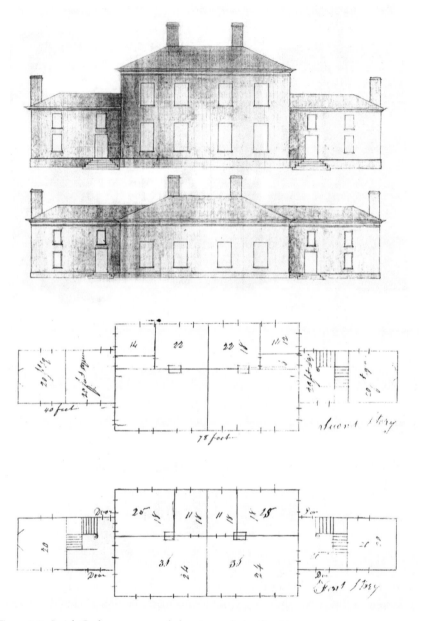

Figure 2.9. Josiah Cushman, proposed elevation and plan for either a one- or two-storey centre building flanked, as wings, by the rebuilt first Parliament buildings, 22 March 1819. *(NAC
NMC-RG 1, E3, v.99. p.110)*

I have the honor to report to you for the information of His Excellency the Lieutenant Governor, the destruction this morning of the main body & the north wing of the Parliament House. The fire appears to have originated in the north wing occupied as my office and committee rooms, and before the alarm was made general (between one & two o'clock) to have involved in flame the whole of the interior of that wing so that not the smallest article pertaining to the Assembly Office escaped.

The Library I am happy to say has sustained but little damage, and the furniture of both the Legislative Chambers with the entree of the office of the Legislative Council has been preserved with no more injury than is unavoidably attendant on such a disaster.

Measures have been taken for the security of the property rescued from the flames, and adopting your suggestion offered on the spot, I have directed its removal into the vacant apartment of the Hospital as a temporary shelter until the pleasure of His Excellency is known (Firth 1966:17).

The loss was estimated to be in the neighbourhood of £2,000 and according to the *Canadian Review* "in the present state of the finances and debt of the Province, cannot be considered a trifling affair" (Scadding 1966:3). It is noteworthy that, in 1825, rewards were offered for those arriving first at a fire with "puncheon or barrels" of water and for those continuing to assist in bringing water in the form of £15 for the first cart, £10 for the second, and £5 for the third. By 1826, Parliament had passed an act for "the more effectual provision for the prevention of accidents by fire" by establishing a 25-member volunteer fire brigade (Jones 1924:134–135).

Dereliction and Demolition, 1824–1830

The accidental destruction of the second Parliament buildings forced the Legislative Assembly to hold its sittings in the vacant hospital near the northwest corner of King and John streets. The hospital had been completed in 1819, but could not be furnished or staffed for lack of funds (Firth 1966:xii, Dale 1993:15–17). Following its re-appropriation by the hospital in 1829, the Legislature moved to the York Court House. It would never again sit on Parliament Street.

A select committee of the House of Assembly was appointed in 1826 to investigate alternative accommodations. It recommended that

> it would not be advisable to attempt repairing the parliament house, which has been destroyed by fire … [and] injudicious to apply so considerable a sum of money as would be necessary in the attempt to repair a building of which the remaining walls might not be found to be of much value (Firth 1966:20).

Apparently, this view prevailed even when it was acknowledged that the cost of a new building "might somewhat exceed" the £7,000 provided by an act of the Legislature in 1826 (Firth 1966:22). Seventy residents from the area surrounding the former Parliament site signed a petition dated 16 January 1829 opposing a capital expenditure to erect new Parliament buildings on the west side of town when less could be spent restoring the former Parliament buildings (Firth 1966:31). While an eye to government costs may have been the stated rationale behind the petition, it is likely that the underlying motive was the potential loss to investments in property and buildings in the area.

One year later, on 11 February 1830, a counter-petition was submitted by 220 inhabitants of York expressing their support for building at Simcoe Place (Front Street, between John and Simcoe streets). They cited the inconvenience and unhealthiness of the old site. Moreover, they argued that the cost of repairing the old buildings would not be realized in the case of sale (moving the seat of Government from York was again threatened), for "no person having a regard to health would select it for a residence — the untenanted State of houses adjoining the … Marsh, confirm them in this opinion" (Firth 1966:30). Proponents for the western site prevailed. The third Parliament buildings of Upper Canada were built at Simcoe Place at a cost in excess of £10,000 between 1820 and 1832. The first session was convened in the new chambers on 31 October 1832.

The second Parliament buildings continued to stand a few years longer (Plate 4), and although ruinous, they were inhabited. A series of letters written between December 1826 and January 1828 described the temporary residency of Samuel Chearnley and family in the buildings, starting in the winter of 1826. Chearnley perhaps felt he could appeal directly to Lieutenant Governor Maitland to aid his homeless family, because Chearnley's daughter, Jane Hall, was a servant to Lady Sarah Maitland.

On 2 December 1826, the 71-year-old Chearnley asked Maitland for lodging in York, imploring that he be allowed to sleep somewhere indoors. Maitland's response has not survived, but on 10 January, Chearnley wrote to Major Hillier that his family was lodged in a room in the old Parliament, and he requested a half dozen old cast bedcases because they were sleeping on the floor (Upper Canada Sundries 1826).

The Lieutenant Governor evicted Chearnley in 1827. Chearnley moved to Niagara, having requested the use of an empty barracks at Fort George. But at all times he was intent on returning to York and felt that he had earned a place in the derelict second Parliament buildings. He lobbied Major Hillier in a letter dated 6 August 1827 that he had whitewashed and cleaned the "vile and nauseous mess" that had existed at the Parliament buildings when he first arrived. Continuing his efforts in a letter from Niagara on 1 January 1828, he again described the improvements he had made during the thirteen months he occupied the building(s), from 4 November 1826 (the dates of the letters and stated period of occupation are not in complete agreement). His labour included:

> cleansing the interior, building a fireplace in a room where none was before, the highly disgusting job of erasing indecencies from the walls and getting the walls whitewashed twice, barricading the windows which were open to the weather, putting up new doors, and taking special care of the whole house so that the abominable and disgraceful orgies and midnight revels were stopped (Upper Canada Sundries 1828).

Samuel Chearnley died on 1 September 1828, unsuccessful in his attempt to appropriate the remaining south wing of the old Parliament for his family's personal use. The building remained empty until its demolition.

The fate of the second Parliament buildings of Upper Canada was sealed in 1830. An Executive Council report of 22 March 1830 recommended materials from the derelict Parliament building be sold by public auction, noting that the walls were falling to ruin and bricks and stone were being taken away by persons in the neighbourhood (Upper Canada State Papers 1830). On 1 April 1830, the *Colonial Advocate* advertised that the sale would take place "Monday next [April 5] by auction on the spot."

The property remained vacant until 1837 when the Home District Gaol was constructed there.

Home District Gaol, 1838–1864

The first gaol in York was a squat, unpainted, wooden log stockade built, circa 1798, on a wooded lot on King Street, east of Yonge. People were imprisoned more readily than today, and the gaols housed "criminals, lunatics, women, children, debtors, and untried persons" (Jones 1924:48). The second gaol, located on the north side of King Street, between Toronto and Church streets, was a two-storey brick structure plagued with management and security problems. Men, women, and children often shared the same space; and convicted felons, the mentally ill, and debtors were incarcerated together. The gaol wall was in such bad repair that the gaoler could not permit the prisoners to have access to the yard for fear of escapes (Talbot 1983:244–250).

Toronto's third gaol was a substantial limestone structure built for the Home District between 1838 and 1840, on the site of the former Parliament buildings. Although there was modest prison reform in Europe at the time, such ideas lacked public support in Upper Canada (Oliver 1998:81–85). As a result, the Home District Gaol incorporated few progressive features and was often described in unflattering terms:

> The architecture of this third gaol was such that prisoners could not see the earth, and saw but little of 'that little tent of blue which prisoners call the sky' and 'each man trembled as he crept into his numbered tomb' ... . Round this third Toronto gaol was a twelve foot wall on which at times a scaffold was erected so that due publicity might be given to hangings (Jones 1924:64).

> Toronto's third jail looked like a stone mausoleum bunker. A drawing of this prison indicates a series of eight small windows on each floor on the side wing capped by a circular head, and one can imagine the dark corridors within (Talbot 1983:250).

> If anything, this prison was more terrifying than the old Newgate, whose demolition in 1911 was the cause for general rejoicing in London (Arthur 1986:79).

In Upper Canada, typically, the gaol was supervised by a government-appointed sheriff. Often the gaoler and his family lived on the premises. He was aided by one of two assistant gaolers called turnkeys (Talbot 1983:283).

In 1846, the Home District Gaol had a gaoler and three turnkeys to oversee 70 prisoners. In 1854, a fourth turnkey and a matron were added; by 1859 two more turnkeys had been hired (Jones 1924:92–93).

Construction, 1837–1840

In response to a call for designs in 1837 for the Home District Court House and Gaol, John Howard submitted two sets of plans, one of which secured the first premium in the competition (Morriss 1982b:132). Subject to certain modifications, his design for a gaol with three radiating three-storey wings around an octagonal five-storey central tower (Figure 2.10) was accepted.

Messrs McLeod and Logan of Kingston built the structure between 1837 and 1840. Although the original plans have not survived, it is thought that the materials used in the construction were limestone and brick (Home District Quarter Session Minutes 1837–1841).

In July 1837, the building committee was authorized to begin excavations for the foundation walls. By October of that year, the foundation of the gaoler's house and the drains had been completed, as were the gaol's foundation walls and a portion of the cut stone and brick work. By August 1838, the centre building was ready to be roofed. At that time a contract was signed for the construction of the west and south wings, which called for their completion by November 1838 and July 1839, respectively. The cost of these wings was set at £5,950, exclusive of iron, lumber, and tin. To date, the new gaol had cost £9,657/15/5.

On 6 July 1839 construction was suspended for a brief time, "on account of Messrs McLeod and Logan's bad Work in Arches &c &c" (Morriss, 1982b:192). Howard's report of 20 December 1839 to the Building Committee noted that the contractors had failed to complete the two wings, as requested, because of a lack of funds. To save costs the committee decided to substitute brick for stone in the division walls between the cells. While the boundary walls still had to be built, Howard was confident that the gaol would be ready for occupation by the summer of 1840 (Home District Quarter Session Minutes 1837–1841). The names of the suppliers and costs of some of the gaol's hardware can be found in Howard's journals (Morriss 1982a, Morriss 1982b) such as gate hinges ($6 a pair), and the weathercock ($30), which was made by Paul Bishop, a blacksmith located at Caroline and Duke streets).

Figure 2.10. John G. Howard, *Courthouse and Gaol,* circa 1836. *(TL T-11968)* The court house, to the left of the complex, was never built.

In March 1840, the District Magistrates granted an additional £3,000 for construction. (Morriss 1982b:19). Howard noted in his journal on 3 August 1840 that he had completed the plan for the gaol privies and gaol wall. With the exception of some minor outbuildings and one of the three planned wings, it appears that the gaol was completed that fall and was used until 1860 (Figures 2.11 and 2.12). In the end, neither the court house nor the third (eastern) wing of the gaol were ever built.

Reuse of the Home District Gaol, 1860–1887

While the Home District Gaol closed in 1860, it remained standing for more than twenty-five years. By 1865, however, no new use had been found for the building and it began to pose problems. Snow came in through the windows and trespassers were able to enter the grounds through the unsecured eastern gate.

In 1866–1867, military authorities leased the property for the confinement of prisoners convicted in connection with the Fenian raids. About the same time, the grounds were rented to a Mr. Williams for cultivation, an arrangement that continued for a number of years (Council of the Corporation of the United Counties of York and Peel 1864–1868).

In June 1868, the *Globe and Leader* advertised that the gaol and property were for sale at a set price of $20,000. The only offer received was for half that amount and it was refused. A year later, a request to use the former gaol as a reformatory prison or house of refuge was granted, however, this plan did not materialize. In 1870, a number of repairs were made to the again vacant

Figure 2.11. Owen Staples, sketch of the Home District Gaol, circa 1850. *(TL T-12031)*

Figure 2.12. Detail from a photograph taken from the tower at St. James' Cathedral (facing east) showing the Home District Gaol, circa 1874. *(St. James' Cathedral Archives)*

and "seriously dilapidated" building, that included replacing broken windows and stone eavestroughs. It was also ordered that "the gates be secured to keep wanton persons out" (Council of the Corporation of the United Counties of York and Peel 1869–1870).

On 4 February 1870, a committee of County Council recommended relinquishing to the Toronto and Nipissing Railway Company an area of the gaol grounds "south of a line parallel to Palace Street [Front Street] one hundred feet south of the gaol building, together with water lots; and the lease of an additional 40 feet on a 42 year lease on condition no buildings be built thereon" (Council of the Corporation of the United Counties of York and Peel 1869–1870). Later that year, a portion of the gaol yard was leased to William Hamilton & Son's, whose foundry was located directly across Front Street. At that time, it was recommended that the stone gutters be covered with zinc or galvanized iron to prevent water from the roof from destroying the building's walls (Council of the Corporation of the United Counties of York and Peel 1869–1870). In the latter 1870s, the building was rented briefly by the J.J. Taylor Safe Company, which had its main office further east on Front Street. It is not known how the company made use of the vacant gaol.

Demolition, circa 1887

The Consumers' Gas Company purchased the property, circa 1879. It is not known if Consumers' Gas ever made use of the gaol before demolishing it in 1887, to facilitate an expansion of its operations along Parliament Street. Figure 2.13 shows the south wing of the gaol during demolition.

Consumers' Gas Company Station A, 1884–1963

The Consumers' Gas Company of Toronto was incorporated in 1848 and began to manufacture coal gas shortly afterwards (Warrington and Nicholls 1949:115). The gasworks were located on the east side of Parliament Street, south of Front Street (Boulton 1858). By 1910, the gasworks had reached its maximum size, covering about two and a half city blocks, extending along the south side of Front Street from west of Berkeley to Trinity Street. The company

Figure 2.13. "The Old Gaol at the foot of Berkeley Street in the process of demolition," circa 1887, south wing. *(TL T-34901)*

also had two gas purifier buildings on the north side of Front, at Parliament Street. Around this time the Front Street gasworks had become known as the Station "A" plant, to distinguish it from the Station "B" gasworks at Eastern Avenue and Booth Street, completed in 1909.

During the latter nineteenth and early twentieth centuries, Station A was expanded and modernized to increase capacity to meet the growing demands of Toronto. In 1887, the company purchased additional lots, which enabled output to increase from two million to eight million cubic feet per day. A new retort house and associated buildings were built on the Parliament site. The initial work was completed in 1888–1889, and the first gas was manufactured in the new plant in June 1889 (Consumers' Gas Company 1887–1940: 1887, 1888, 1889).

By 1890, Consumers' Gas produced lighting and heating gas by two methods. The older method, used since the company first manufactured gas, was coal gasification. The company added a water gas plant during the 1880s and, by 1900, the Station A gasworks had evolved into two distinct plants — one for the manufacture of coal gas and one for water gas. Ultimately, the production of coal and water gases was about equal. In the late 1940s, the coal gasworks produced seven million cubic feet per day, while the water gasworks produced 7.5 million cubic feet (Tucker 1948). The two processes yielded virtually identical gases that were mixed after the final purification process (Stewart 1958:30–31).

As Toronto grew in the early twentieth century, Station A could no longer satisfy the demand for manufactured gas. Since expanding Station A was impossible, Consumers' Gas developed a new site, Station B, on Eastern Avenue. When completed in 1909, it added four million cubic feet to the system (Tucker 1948). The opening of Station B enabled the company to shut down parts of Station A in 1908–1909, and to rebuild the entire coal gas facility. In 1924, the company again embarked on a program to rebuild the Station A coal gas plant (Consumers' Gas Company 1887–1940:1924–1925).

Consumers' Gas closed its coal gas manufacturing facilities and became a natural gas retailing operation when natural gas became available in Toronto during the 1950s. Today, the only surviving buildings of the gasworks are the former coal gas purifying building, now the Canadian Opera Company, and the water gas purifying building at the northeast corner of Parliament and Front streets, slated to become a City of Toronto police division headquarters.

Construction Activities

William Hamilton & Son's St. Lawrence Foundry, which had a large works on the north side of Front Street, also had a workshop on the south side of Front Street, somewhere between Berkeley and Parliament streets, by 1876. As well, the Toronto and Nipissing Railway had several rail spurs, a turntable, and associated sheds on the southern and western parts of the property. By 1878, the workshop was unoccupied, and one year later, Consumers' Gas used the land along Parliament Street, next to the former gaol, as a coke yard (Figure 2.14).

The existence of the vacant gaol at the time of expansion of the gasworks affected the siting of the gasworks buildings. The gaol sat in the centre of the lot, so gasworks facilities were located around it, close to the edges of the property. For example, the coke shed was located along Parliament Street and a coal shed appears to have been added to the existing coke shed in 1881 (Figure 2.15). Coal was dumped from rail cars at the south end of the building and moved by conveyor into the shed. The coal shed supplied both the coal gas and water gas plants (City of Toronto Directories 1876–1881, Consumers' Gas Company 1887–1940:1887, 1888, 1889).

The balance of the gaol was demolished in 1887 when Consumers' Gas decided to build its retort house, leaving a central courtyard around which encircled the subsequent constructions. The coal gas retort house of 1888–1889 defined the west side of the courtyard (Consumers' Gas Company 1887–1940:1887, 1888, 1889). A large, brick office building, built in the early 1890s along Front Street, defined the north edge of the courtyard; it was completely rebuilt in 1899 and was still standing as late as 1954 (Figures 2.16 and 2.17) (Consumers' Gas Company 1887–1940:1889).

The southern end of the courtyard was open to the railway yards. The narrow gauge Toronto & Nipissing Railway built its Toronto terminal in 1871 on vacant land south of the gaol. The railway's roundhouse and turntable were immediately south of the area later occupied by the Consumers' Gas coal shed on Parliament Street (Lavallee 1972:12–13) (Figures 2.14 and 2.15).

Courtyard Features

Courtyard

The function of the Consumers' Gas courtyard is as yet unknown. The fact that it existed at all seems to have been due to the presence of the gaol when the coal shed and retort house were constructed. As the gasworks grew, the company's property became crowded with buildings, except for this large yard, which circumstantial evidence shows was useful to the operation of the plant. In the 1890s, for example, when a site was needed for a water gas purifying building, new land was purchased on the north side of Front Street, rather than using the vacant yard.

Although a rail line crossed the courtyard, the area was not used for the delivery of coal or oil. Coal was delivered by rail car to the south end of the coal shed, while oil was unloaded from tank cars in the rail yard south of the courtyard. Nor was the courtyard used for the shipment of coal tar; tar was loaded at special tracks in the rail yard. In the 1920s, a portion of the courtyard adjacent to the rail line was planked. It appears that the courtyard was generally kept clear of equipment and materials (Figures 2.18–2.20). By the mid-twentieth century the courtyard had been paved with concrete (Underwriters Survey Bureau 1954).

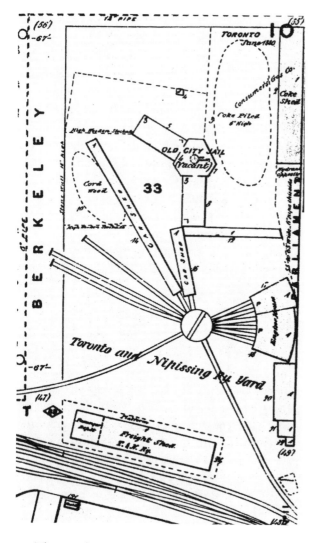

Figure 2.14. Detail from C.E. Goad, *Goad's Insurance Plan*, 1880, showing the old gaol, the Toronto and Nipissing Railway yard and spurs, and the Consumers' Gas coke shed and coke pile (noted as six feet high).

The northern part of the courtyard, containing the scale building, may have been used for teams of wagons picking up coke, while the remainder of the yard was for general works.

There are several possible reasons for the avoidance of major construction in the courtyard. It may simply have been too expensive to remove the rather substantial gaol foundation in that area and the area would have therefore functioned as an effective firebreak between the retort house and the coal shed.

Figure 2.15. Detail from
C.E. Goad, *Atlas of the
City of Toronto and sub-
urbs,* 1884, showing the
old gaol, the Consum-
ers' Gas coal shed, and
the Midland Railway
yard.

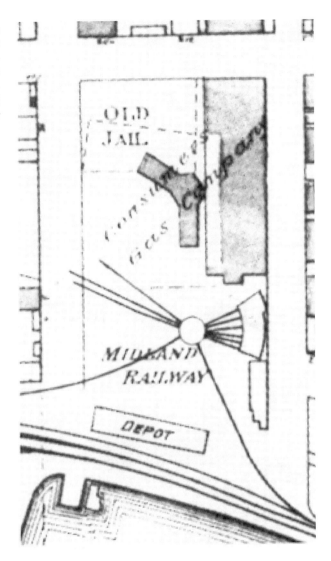

Rail Line

The purpose of the rail line across the yard has not been determined. It does
not seem to have been used regularly. The grade of the track appears to have
been below the level of the yard. The depressed track would have placed car
doors level with the yard and facilitated loading and unloading rail cars. The
track was used on occasion to bring in construction material. It might also
have been used for the occasional bulk shipment.

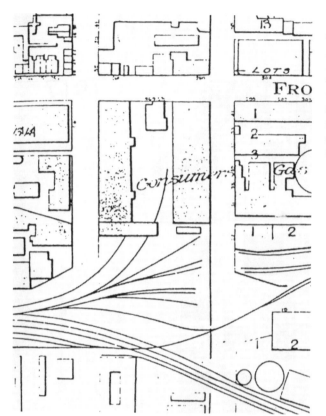

Figure 2.16. Detail from C.E. Goad, *Goad's Atlas of the City of Toronto and suburbs*, 1910, showing the Consumers' Gas coal shed (east side of property), the retort building (west side), the office structure (north side), and the rail spur into the courtyard.

Retort House/Stores Building

Coal gas was manufactured by carbonizing coal in airtight retorts. This process produced two major products, coal gas and coke, and numerous commercial by-products, including coal tar, benzene, toluene, and ammonia. Some of the coke was used subsequently to heat the retorts in which the coal gas and coke was made, while the rest was sold.

Coal retorts had been used since the opening of the gasworks in the late 1840s. The date of construction of the retort house on Berkeley Street, adjacent to the courtyard, was not confirmed but the retort house appears to have been built in 1888–1889 (Consumers' Gas Company 1887–1940: 1887, 1888, 1889). The original types of retorts used in the works were not determined. However, in 1925–1926, eight settings of Glover-West vertical retorts were installed (Consumers' Gas Company 1887–1940:1924, 1925, 1927). This design was a continuous, vertical retort that had been perfected in the

Figure 2.17. Detail from Underwriters Survey Bureau, *Fire Insurance Plans for Toronto*, 1954, showing the courtyard in relation to the retort house, office building, coal and coke shed and conveyors, the scale building, and the rail yard in the 1950s.

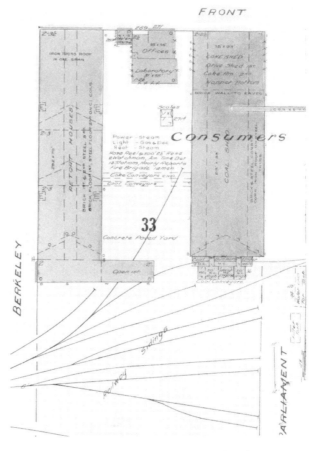

early twentieth century and was much more efficient than the batch, or intermittent, retorts then in use (Stewart 1958:16–17).

At the south end of the retort house was a building described as "stores." This structure appears to have been added after the retort house was built. The second floor of this building projected across the courtyard and was elevated above two railway tracks by supporting piers (Figure 2.17).

Scale House

A small frame scale house was located near the coke shed. The building was presumably used to weigh wagonloads of coke. Since there were no ramps at either entrance to the scales, the weigh bridge would have been in a pit below yard level.

Figure 2.18. Consumers' Gas Station A, circa 1950. *(Courtesy Toronto Sun collection, M. Filey)*

Figure 2.19. View of the courtyard looking northeast towards Front Street, circa 1930, showing the corner of the administration building, coal shed, scale house, coal conveyors, depressed rail track, and the relatively clean yard. *(TA, Consumers' Gas photographic collection SC34-764)*

Figure 2.20. View from the courtyard looking northwest towards Front Street, circa 1930. Note the concrete footings for the conveyor trestles. *(TA, Consumers' Gas photographic collection, SC34-361)*

Coal- and Coke-Conveying Equipment

Coal was initially carted from the coal shed, across the courtyard, to the retort house. In 1901, coal- and coke-conveying machinery was erected to connect the two buildings (Consumers' Gas Company 1887–1940:1901). The conveyors were located at the north end of the yard, adjacent to the scale house. New coal and coke conveyors were installed further south when the Glover-West retorts were added in the 1920s. The old conveyors were removed. While the original conveyors had been supported on steel bents with no visible concrete footings, the bents of the new conveyors were installed on massive concrete footings (Figures 2.19 and 2.20).

Buried Utilities

Considering the complexity of piping associated with coal gas manufacturing, surprisingly few conduits passed under the courtyard. Coal gas from the retort house crossed under Berkeley Street to the purifying building. Cleaned gas came back east along Front Street to a meter house in the administration building. The gas mains then continued along Front to gasholders at Trinity and Front streets.

Four pipes of unknown function cut across the yard from the coal shed to the retort house, a few metres south of and parallel to the administration building. These pipes probably carried water and steam. Sewer or drainage pipes ran parallel to the retort house and coal shed, and one line cut across the south end of the courtyard.

Consumers' Gas Commemoration of the Parliament Buildings

The Parliament site was commemorated in 1934 by Consumers' Gas, noting that the company "remembers, not without pride, that it occupies at the southern end of Berkeley Street, the site of the first Parliament buildings, for long years the heart of Upper Canada" (Middleton 1934:186). Even earlier, in 1899, the Canadian Club had erected a stone tablet outside the Front Street entrance to Station A (Consumers' Gas Company 1954) that read:

> This tablet marks the north east corner
> of the First Legislative Buildings
> of the Province of Upper Canada completed in
> 1797 under Lieut. Governor Simcoe
> burnt by the American troops April 27, 1813.
> Here also stood the Second Legislative Buildings 1818–24
> accidentally burnt 1824
> and Third Toronto Gaol 1840–60.

The current whereabouts of the tablet is unknown.

Destruction, 1960–1964

After coal gas production ceased in the 1950s, all the buildings in the block, bounded by Berkeley, Front, and Parliament streets, were demolished by the early 1960s. The Consumers' Gas Company sold the property in 1964. No records have been found that provide the exact date of the demolition of the buildings.

Recent Land Uses, 1964–2001

The current uses of the Parliament site date back to the mid-1960s. There has been a relatively consistent mixture of automotive-related businesses there over the thirty-seven-year period. Figure 2.21 shows the configuration of the two Front Street properties and the Berkeley Street lot that compose the Parliament site. The structures housing the commercial enterprises on the property are documented in two photographs taken in 1973 (Figures 2.22 and 2.23).

Figure 2.21. The configuration of the three properties bounded by Front, Berkeley, and Parliament streets.

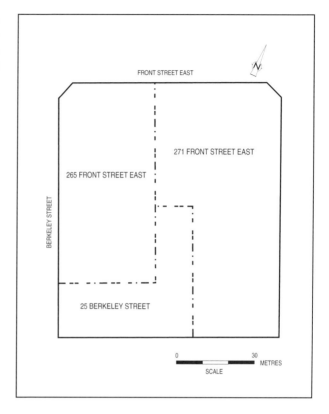

265 Front Street East

Beginning in 1964, two businesses operated at 265 Front Street: Dimont T Trucks and Front Truck Servicentre Ltd. The extant cinder block structure likely dates to 1964, with minor alterations over time. By 1970, Atlas Auto Leasing and the Addison Chevrolet Olds Ltd. body shop also operated from the same address. In 1974, the Don Valley Truck Wash was built, comprising the narrow structure adjacent to the existing building (although listed as 265 Front Street East, the structure is situated on 271 Front Street East on current plans). The ownership and names of the body shop and car wash changed a number of times until Fuhrman Auto Body opened in 1985, later called Fuhrman Autocentre. Fuhrman closed in 1999 and both the auto service centre and truck wash structures remain empty.

In 1999, a set of gas tanks, located in the northwest corner of the property at 265 Front Street, was removed. The excavation apparently revealed the

Figure 2.22. View of the Fina Station, facing west. 271 Front Street East is in the foreground, 1973. *(TL RG 230-5)*

Figure 2.23. View of the north half of 271 Front Street East, facing west, 1973. *(TL RG 230-3)*

remains of two brick interior walls from the Consumers' Gas retort house. Mr. Heinz Furhman reported that other previous disturbances on the property had brought to light another set of underground tanks to the south of the automotive centre that would have been situated within the footprint of the retort building. He has also indicated that a rail spur is located underneath the asphalt surface at the rear of the property. The rail spur is likely the line for the Toronto and Nipissing rail yard car shed (Figure 2.16).

271 Front Street East

In 1964, Dash Auto Centres Ltd., Motorcade Stores Ltd., and the Dash Restaurant were built on the property. They likely occupied the cinder block structure that was renovated to accommodate a Dash Car Wash in 1967 or 1968. By 1973, a Fina Gas Service Bar was located on the northwestern part of the lot, facing Front Street (Figure 2.22), and was demolished after 1980. The site has had several owners in the 1980s, with little modification to the property. Budget Rent-A-Car and the Executive Car Wash currently use the property.

25 Berkeley Street

There are no records for businesses ever having been registered at 25 Berkeley Street. The address refers to the L-shaped property that serves currently as a car rental agency parking lot. No construction activities have occurred on the lot since the Consumers' Gas structures were demolished.

3

KNOWING WHERE TO DIG

The potential for recovering evidence of the first and second Parliament buildings was initially believed to be very low due to the extensive post-1830 construction history of the site. An overlay of historic maps was conducted prior to the excavations to determine where the best opportunities would lie for the recovery of parliamentary-era materials (see The Citizens for the Old Town n.d.). In the interests of time and expediency, this overlay was used as the basis for the test excavations and proved to be an effective guide to the archaeological work.

Simply, the best opportunity for the survival of parliamentary remnants would be in areas where no subsequent construction had ever overlain the ruins of the former Parliament buildings. Three areas within the property met that criterion. The courtyard between the coal/coke storage and retort buildings was the largest and had the highest potential. Apart from the rail line, scale house, footings for the conveyor systems, and buried drains and utility piping (all relatively minor), no construction work seemed to have occurred in this area. The fact that the yard was paved would have helped to cap any significant deposits, assuming that the grade had not been lowered substantially.

Two small areas of possibly undisturbed land existed close to Front Street, to the east and west of the former Consumers' Gas administrative building. These areas seem to have had land use histories similar to that of the main courtyard.

Following the excavations, a more detailed examination of the history of the Front Street properties was conducted using a series of maps and plans dating from 1805 to 1990. This led to a refinement of our understanding of both the former locations of the Parliament buildings, of subsequent nineteenth and early twentieth century structures, and of the area of highest potential for still-intact parliamentary-era deposits.

Historic map overlays were produced to determine the extent of potentially undisturbed parliamentary-era remains among the footprints of the

Third Gaol, Consumers' Gas structures, and extant buildings. Those historic maps showing the first Parliament buildings were D.W. Smith (1805), S. Wilmot (1810), and S. Smith (1819). The utility of the earliest of these maps, Smith's 1805 *Sketch of Mr. Small's Improvements,* in predicting the location of the first Parliament buildings, had been examined previously by Eva MacDonald, of ASI, on behalf of the Toronto Historical Board (Archaeological Services Inc. 1989). A single source, J.G. Chewett (1830), shows the second Parliament building. Plans by Williams (1813, 1814) and Nicolls (1816), among others, were not used due to their smaller scale. The 1805 D.W. Smith overlay is shown on Figure 3.1, the 1810 Wilmot overlay on Figure 3.2, the 1819 S. Smith overlay on Figure 3.3, and the 1830 Chewett overlay on Figure 3.4.

For the District Gaol, a broken selection of plans was available. Those by W. Kingsford (1855) and Browne and Browne (1862) were used, as were two plans prepared by C.E. Goad (1880, 1884) when the structure was under the ownership of Consumers' Gas. The Kingsford overlay is shown on Figure 3.5. The location of the District Gaol is most accurately depicted in relation to Berkeley, Parliament, and Front streets, and to the Consumers' Gas coke shed on the 1884 plan (Figures 2.14 and 2.15).

Consumers' Gas structure overlays were taken from the 1884 Goad plan as well as the 1899 and 1910 Goad Plans and a detailed Consumers' Gas plan (undated, circa 1920–1930). The Consumers' Gas overlays are shown on Figures 3.6 and 3.7. Finally, the plan of post-Consumers' Gas structures comprising the former automotive centre and truck wash at 265 Front Street and modern car wash at 271 Front Street was used as a modern-day overlay.

The basic reference points used in all of the overlays were the centre points of the intersections of Berkeley, Front, and Parliament streets. The choice of this approach was premised on the assumption that these centre points are likely to have remained more or less constant, whereas the corners of intersections are likely to have changed through time due to road widenings and flanking redevelopment. As is the case with all such mapping exercises, there are numerous potential sources of error, but given the size of the Parliament building envelope so created, relative to the overall property, these errors are unlikely to be unduly significant.

The four depictions, circa 1805–1830, of the Parliament buildings were simultaneously overlaid and an envelope was then drawn encompassing all of the depicted structures (Figure 3.8). This envelope represents the relative maximum area of potential for the recovery of archaeological material for parliamentary-era buildings. The parliamentary envelope was then overlaid on each of the plans for the District Gaol, Consumers' Gas, and current structures. All structures, or portions thereof, situated within the Parliament building envelope, were noted as areas of post-1830 disturbance. These areas were subsequently marked as probable zones of disturbance within the parliamentary envelope and eliminated from consideration. However, significant areas remain that have not undergone any major (or at least documented) post-1830 disturbances.

The historic-map overlays yielded a zone that encompasses the former Parliament buildings and that was documented as void of significant construction activities after 1830. This zone has the greatest likelihood for the recovery of archaeological evidence pertaining to the use of the property between 1796 and 1830.

Figures 3.9 and 3.10 depict the Parliament buildings envelope, the potential zone, the location of the 2000 test trench excavations, and extant structures.

Briefly, two of the three archaeological test trenches did not result in the recovery of any parliamentary-era materials. The historic maps overlays indicated that these two trenches had actually been placed in areas of post-1830 disturbance (Figures 3.9 and 3.10). In contrast, the test trench excavations in which parliamentary-era material was recovered (in the courtyard) was situated within an undisturbed zone. A detailed discussion of the excavations is presented in the next chapter.

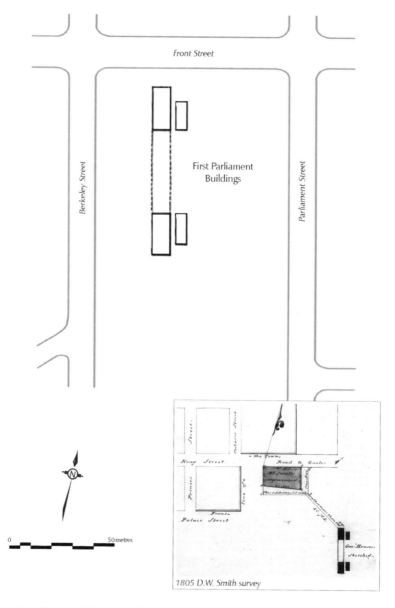

Figure 3.1. Overlay of the 1805 D.W. Smith survey and the current street plan (the first Parliament buildings are labelled "Govt Houses – sketched" on the 1805 survey).

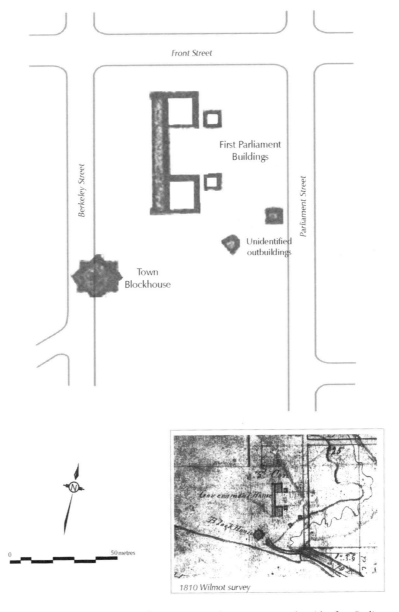

Figure 3.2. Overlay of the 1810 Wilmot survey and current street plan (the first Parliament buildings are labelled "Government House" on the 1810 survey).

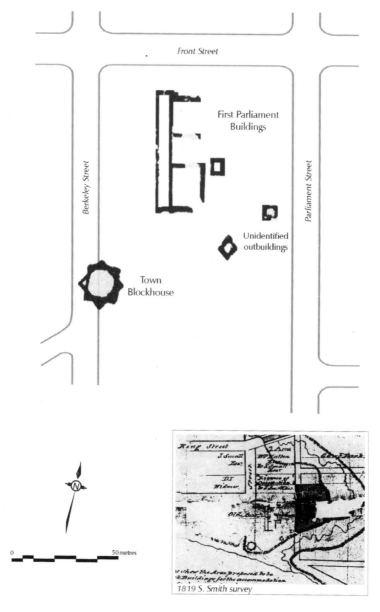

Figure 3.3. Overlay of the 1819 S. Smith survey and current street plan (the first Parliament buildings are labelled "Old Gov't Buildings" on the 1819 plan).

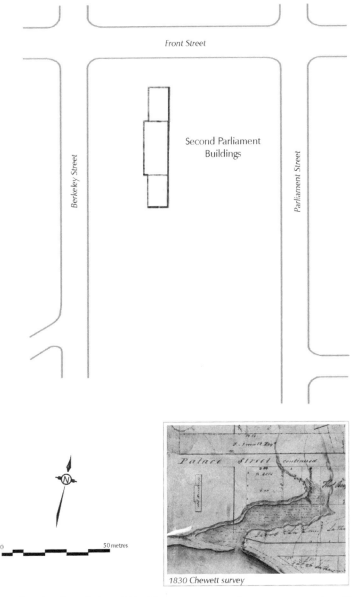

Figure 3.4. Overlay of the 1830 Chewett survey and current street plan (the second Parliament buildings are labelled "Old Buildings" on the 1830 plan).

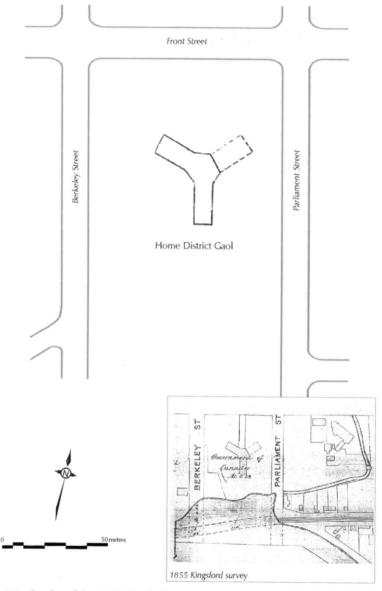

Figure 3.5. Overlay of the 1855 Kingsford survey and current street plan (the Home District Gaol is labelled "Government of Canada" on the 1855 survey).

Plate 9. ASI archaeological team taking a well-deserved coffee break: (left to right) Ronald Williamson, Debbie Steiss, Irena Miklavcic, Stephen Monckton, Andrew Clish, and Frank Dieterman.

Plate 10. Rollo Myers, Parliament site co-ordinator with The Citizens for the Old Town (left), being interviewed by Kelly McKeown (seated at right) of the Discovery Channel.

Plate 11. City of Toronto, provincial, and federal politicians visiting the Parliament site: (left to right) Archaeological Services Inc.'s Chief Archaeologist Ronald Williamson; Member of Provincial Parliament Rosario Marchese; Toronto City Councillor Pam McConnell; Member of Provincial Parliament George Smitherman; and Member of Parliament Bill Graham.

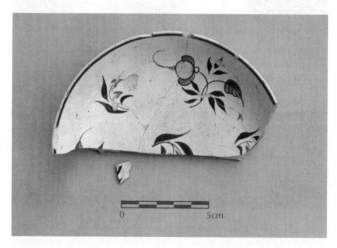

Plate 12. Creamware with early palette hand-painted decoration: saucer from Fort York (upper), and a sherd from original topsoil, Parliament buildings site (lower).

Plate 13. Detail of the north-south limestone footing at 75-centimetres depth.

Plate 14. The partial excavation of Feature 2, showing the charcoal, lime mortar, siltstone flooring, organic topsoil, drain, and sterile subsoil.

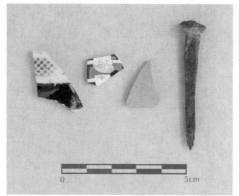

Plate 15. Assorted Feature 2 artifacts. Left panel (left to right): green rouletted pearlware, inlaid slipped creamware, grey stoneware, and hand-wrought nail. Right panel: blackened brick fragment.

Plate 16. Pearlware with monochrome blue hand-painted decoration. Saucer, from the early nineteenth century Flanagan site (upper), and three sherds from similar vessels recovered from Feature 2 at the Parliament buildings site (lower).

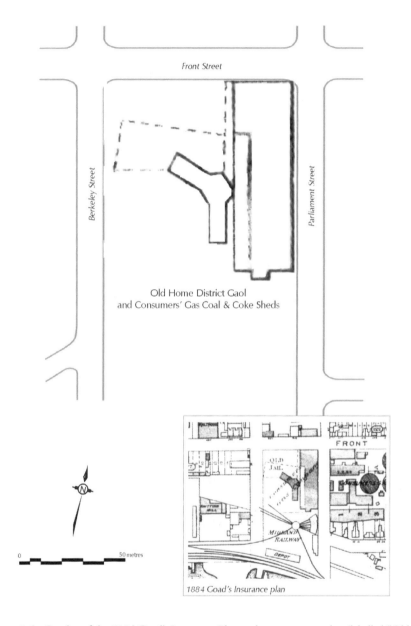

Figure 3.6. Overlay of the 1884 Goad's Insurance Plan and current street plan (labelled "Old Jail & Consumers' Gas Company" on 1884 plan).

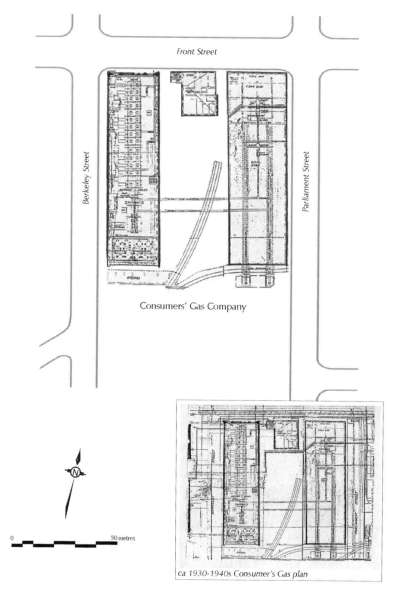

Figure 3.7. Overlay of the 1930s–1940s Consumers' Gas plan and current street plan. The retort house fronts Berkeley Street, the administrative offices front Front Street, and the coal and coke shed fronts Parliament Street.

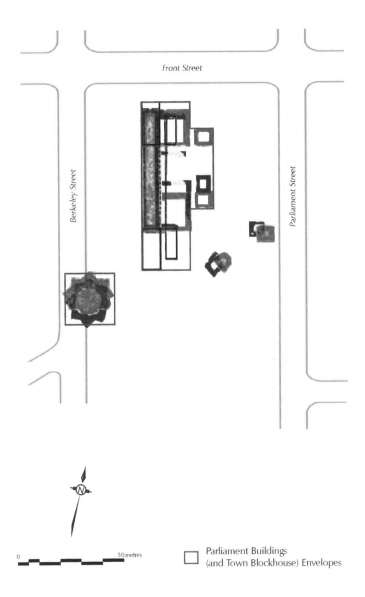

Figure 3.8. Composite overlay of the 1805, 1810, 1819, and 1830 plans and current street plan showing the maximum envelope of the Parliament buildings' footprints.

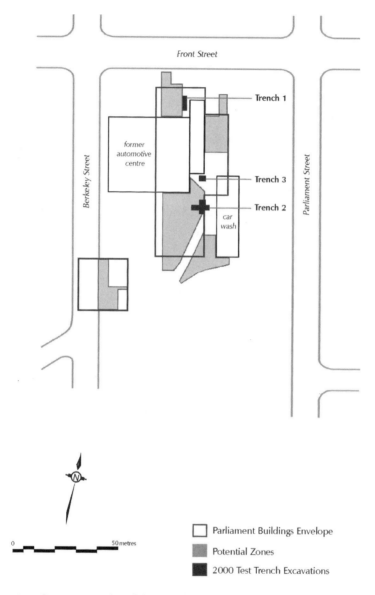

Figure 3.9. Composite overlay of the Parliament buildings envelope, archaeological potential zones, locations of 2000 excavations, and current structures.

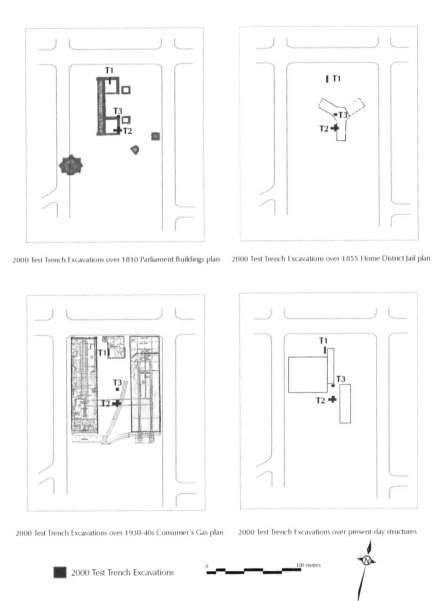

2000 Test Trench Excavations over 1810 Parliament Buildings plan   2000 Test Trench Excavations over 1855 Home District Jail plan

2000 Test Trench Excavations over 1930-40s Consumer's Gas plan   2000 Test Trench Excavations over present-day structures

2000 Test Trench Excavations

0   100 metres

Figure 3.10. Overlay of the 2000 test excavations on the four phases of property occupation.

4

UNCOVERING THE "PALACES OF GOVERNMENT"

By all appearances, the former courtyard of Consumers' Gas, now a parking area, was not the sort of place that one would expect to find evidence of not only the very first brick buildings in the fledgling town of York, but the seat of government itself for all of Upper Canada. Although this was the place that Lieutenant Governor John Graves Simcoe had chosen for the first Parliament buildings, it has long since been forgotten by the burgeoning and bustling city of Toronto. All that remains in the city's collective memory is a street name, Parliament Street, carrying as little historical weight as does Bloor, Jarvis, or Spadina.

Today, if one stands in the middle of this parking area, a few metres to the west lie the vacant shells of an automobile repair shop and truck wash at the corner of Front Street East and Berkeley Street. To the east is a car wash, complete with a full staff to vacuum, polish, and dry vehicles. Quite understandably, the workers at the car wash were sceptical when they were told about the subject of the archaeological search, despite the overlooked irony that their place of employment has a Parliament Street address. Throughout the subsequent few weeks, as happens to most people when witnessing an archaeological excavation, their disbelief turned to inquisitiveness — the question "How do you know it's here?" asked over and over. As the excavation progressed, a sense of ownership prevailed. The workers vowed to keep watch over the site when the archaeologists' days were over. Then, with the evidence before their eyes, they responded with pride and emotion — amateur history buffs emerged, opinions on construction techniques were offered, some found themselves as impromptu tour guides. A few even went so far as to bring their mothers to the site to witness the historic discovery. Today, bragging rights and first-hand accounts rest with the car wash staff.

From the nearly 2,500 artifacts recovered from the excavation areas, what had been found to make believers, not only out of a group of east end workers but also representatives from the City of Toronto and the Province of Ontario, including, in a unique act of symmetry, the present-day Lieutenant Governor Hilary Weston (Plate 5)? In order to answer this question, an understanding of one of the guiding principles of both geology and archaeology is needed. For an archaeologist, the golden rule that is rarely broken is the law of superposition, which simply states that lower levels are believed to be older than upper levels. Having an appreciation of this basic archaeological construct makes it possible to understand the Parliament buildings excavation as interpreted by the archaeologists.

Using historic drawings showing the relative surface levels of the Don River and Lake Ontario, elevation plans of Victorian brick sewers underneath Jarvis and Front Streets, and the existing elevations of surrounding nineteenth-century buildings, it was estimated that any archaeological remains dating to the Parliament buildings era would be encountered at a depth of no greater than 130 centimetres below the present ground surface. The various layers, deposits, and features encountered over the course of the excavation have been summarized in a flow chart (Figure 4.1). Each soil and rubble layer, or man-made feature, was assigned a unique reference number. For this reason, in the following narrative, these numbers do not always follow one another in a logical sequence.

The strategy for excavating in the parking lot was to have a backhoe break through the paved surface and, under the supervision of the archaeological team, expose the earlier levels in each location. One area (Trench 1) was immediately north of the former automotive centre. This trench was located five metres from the north wall of the building and two metres from the west wall of the abandoned truck wash (Figure 4.2 and 4.3). The archaeological investigation then moved to the rear of the property, behind the automotive centre, where two more areas were measured and marked. Trench 2 was located eleven metres south of the automotive building and extended from two metres east of the chain link fence to three metres west of the existing car wash structure. This trench was cross-shaped, with a ten metre by two metre east-west stem and two smaller areas excavated to the north and south (Figure 4.4). The third excavation trench measured three and one-half by four metres and was located one metre south of the former truck wash and four metres from the east wall of the automotive centre (Figure 4.5).

The results of the excavations in the three areas are presented below in sections relating to the various historic construction episodes on the site. These descriptions move back in time, from the present through the Consumers' Gas industrial and Home District Gaol institutional eras to the days when representatives were seated in the newly built "Palaces of Government," Upper Canada's first and second Parliament buildings, both of which met fiery ends.

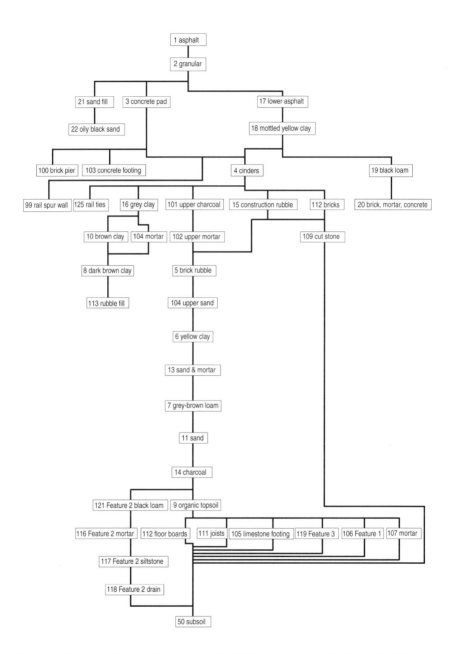

Figure 4.1. Stratigraphic matrix (flow chart) of the 2000 excavations at the Parliament buildings site.

Figure 4.2. Laying out Trench 1, facing northeast; the vacant truck wash wall is to the right.

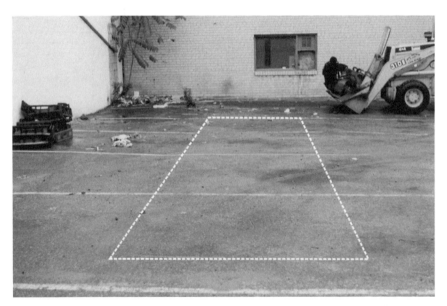

Figure 4.3. Trench 1 outline, facing south; the vacant automotive centre is at the rear.

Figure 4.4. Trench 2 outline, facing south (on the 25 Berkeley Street property).

Figure 4.5. Trench 3 outline, facing north; the vacant truck wash is at the rear.

The Modern Era (Post-1963)

In the excavation area to the north of the automotive centre, the first three stratigraphic layers that were encountered consisted of asphalt (Figure 4.1:#1), granular (Figure 4.1:#2), and a yellow sand fill with occasional inclusions of asphalt fragments (Figure 4.1:#21). Two small steel pipes, cut at their north ends, were found to run diagonally across the test trench. At a depth of nearly two metres below the surface, the yellow sand changed to wet, black-stained sand (Figure 4.1:#22), accompanied by a strong odour of oil. This layer was explored for an additional depth of half a metre, with no change. Faced with uncertainty as to the origin of the oily substance, and the fact that the excavation had far exceeded the estimated depth for intact Parliament building-era deposits, the decision was made to suspend further excavations. Although the backhoe had reached a depth of 220 centimetres below the surface, no artifacts or architectural remains had been found.

The historic map overlay indicates that Test Trench 1 was situated at the western edge of the Consumers' Gas administrative offices on Front Street, and immediately adjacent to an area that has parliamentary-era archaeological potential. The presence of the sand fill and steel pipes, in conjunction with the absence of any materials relating to a late nineteenth century structure, however, indicates that this area has undergone considerable twentieth century modification, obliterating not only parliamentary-era deposits, but also any evidence of subsequent nineteenth or early twentieth century activities. The depth of the post-Consumers' Gas era deposit of clean fill and the underlying presence of the black-stained, oily sand indicates that significant soil removal and fill events have occurred in this area, possibly to address environmental concerns.

The Consumers' Gas Era (1887–1963)

The removal of the surface asphalt and subsequent granular material, in the area immediately south of the automotive centre (Trench 3), revealed a second asphalt surface (Figure 4.1:#17), indicating that, in this vicinity, the lot had been surfaced prior to its current level. Below the asphalt was a layer of yellow clay that contained some red brick and charcoal fragments (Figure 4.1:#18). This layer was more than one metre thick at the south end of the excavation, and half that at the north end. The yellow clay was identified as a fill deposit, given its intermittent and irregular character, the presence of brick and charcoal, and the discovery of a metal pipe approximately 30 centimetres below the asphalt surface.

Directly below the clay was a dense black soil (Figure 4.1:#19) characterized by a slight oily odour and extending, at its deepest, to just over one metre below the surface of the asphalt Within this black soil were found cinders, charcoal, and fragments of bricks and wood. Below the black soil, a mixture of complete and fragmentary bricks, mortar, and fragments of concrete (Figure 4.1:#20) was found at a depth of approximately two metres below the surface. The dense brick rubble was either fill or adjacent to a demolished structure, given the jumbled nature of the bricks. No intact portions of a brick structure were noted.

At this point, at a depth of over two metres, the decision was made again to stop excavations, using the rationale of 130 centimetres as the optimal depth for the recovery of material dating to the Parliament buildings era. Although no definite conclusions could be made regarding the origin of the material recovered from this trench, all of the collected material post-dated the mid-nineteenth century. More importantly, no evidence of parliamentary-era material was observed in this trench.

The historic map overlay indicates that Trench 3 was situated within the area once occupied by the Home District Gaol. Since it is known that the gaol was dismantled to permit Consumers' Gas expansion of activities on the property, the rubble encountered was likely the result of late- nineteenth to early twentieth-century activities associated with the gaol demolition or construction and subsequent demolition of Consumers' Gas structures on the property.

The excavation of Trench 2, the southernmost of the three archaeological test locations, saw the removal of the asphalt and granular, immediately below which there was a thick concrete pad (Figure 4.1:#3), extending over the majority of the exposed area, except for the eastern part of the trench by the car wash wall. At some point during the Consumers' Gas occupation of the property, the narrow courtyard between the gas buildings had been surfaced with concrete.

In addition to the concrete pad, a large, rectangular concrete footing (Figure 4.1:103) was uncovered immediately below the granular (Figure 4.6). This poured concrete block, measuring approximately one metre across, was set into the ground to a depth of at least one metre below the surface. A short length of rebar protruded from its top. Surrounding the block was clear evidence of a builder's trench, filled with yellow clay and brick fragments. Although at first puzzling, the origin of the concrete footing was identified with the aid of historic photos. A number of photos and documents indicate that a set of 1920s Consumers' Gas coal and coke conveyors were supported on steel towers set in concrete footings similar in size and form to the one encountered. Therefore, the concrete footing uncovered in the excavation likely dates to the 1920s. When the concrete pad was poured in the mid-twentieth century by Consumers' Gas, apparently it was easier to work around the concrete footings rather than remove them.

There was no evidence of the concrete pad in the east portion of this excavation trench. Instead, there was a layer of mottled yellow clay containing large blocks of cut limestone, lake cobbles, and stones, and small concrete fragments. This was probably the same layer as was found below the asphalt and granular in the trench immediately south of the automotive centre (Figure 4.1:#18). Additionally, a substantial concrete-faced brick wall (Figure 4.1:#99), nearly one-half-metre thick and extending diagonally across the entire excavation in a southwest to northeast direction, was encountered immediately below the granular (Plate 6). With the aid of historic photos, the wall was identified as a retaining wall for the sunken rail spur that entered the Consumers' Gas courtyard from the south, depicted on historic maps as early

Concrete pad

Top of concrete footing
for Consumers' Gas
coal/coke conveyor

Figure 4.6. Mid-twentieth century concrete pad and 1920s concrete footing in Trench 2.

as 1910. It was constructed of fatigued bricks from the coal retorts and covered by thin concrete facing.

The yellow clay was then excavated, following the rail spur wall. Ten artifacts were found — a single example each of a hand-wrought nail and a wire-cut nail, four indeterminate pieces of iron metal that were too corroded to identify, and four animal bones, two identified as vertebrae from an ox, and a possible sheep leg fragment, all with butcher marks. Nails recovered from archaeological sites are usually assigned unique dates of origin, but have open-ended terminus dates due to the frequent reuse of nails noted during the nineteenth century. The earliest nails are hand-wrought, which are typically square in cross-section, with a four-sided pyramidal head. They were manufactured until circa 1830. Wire-cut nails, characterized by a round or circular cross-section and a round, flat head, are usually associated with twentieth century deposits, although their manufacturing process was developed in the late nineteenth century. Surprisingly, given their usual ubiquity, this wire-cut nail was the only one of its kind found during the entire archaeological excavation.

At a depth of 160 centimetres, the yellow clay gave way to a thick layer of cinders and coal (Figure 4.1:#4). Within this layer, at nearly two metres depth, three undisturbed railway ties were found (Figure 4.1:#125), although the tracks were no longer in place (Figure 4.7). This direct evidence of the sunken rail spur confirmed the identification of the concrete-faced brick wall as the western wall of the rail spur. The small area east of the rail spur, containing the rail ties, was not excavated to any greater depth based on the obvious evidence of extensive early to mid-twentieth century disturbance.

The removal of the concrete pad in the rest of the excavation trench also revealed the thick deposit of coal cinders extending over the entire surface of the trench. A single artifact was observed within this layer; a metal spike measuring 15.2 centimetres in length. It is believed that this deposit originated with the loading of fired coal cinders onto railcars via the sunken rail spur, while the metal spike is obviously related to rail yard activities.

Set amongst the cinders, and clearly marked by builder's trenches, were three small, mortared brick features, identified as brick piers (Figure 4.1:#100). One pier was located immediately west of the concrete footing in the south wall of the excavation (Figure 4.8); a second pier was located in the north wall of the excavation (Figure 4.9), and a third pier, which was only partially intact, as its eastern half had been bisected by the rail spur wall, was located in the middle of the trench (Figure 4.10). The presence of this pier

Figure 4.7. Excavation east of the rail spur concrete wall, showing the railway ties at 170-cm depth.

not only indicated that the spur wall was constructed at a later date than the brick piers, but dated their construction to no later than 1910. The brick piers were of similar design, consisting of a square hollow block, measuring a half metre in length, made of a minimum of seven courses of buff and red bricks measuring 22 by 10 by 6 centimetres (8.5 by 4 by 2.5 inches). The builder's trenches for the piers were cut into the subsoil. Given the size of the well-made bricks, the presence of mortar, and the observation that the builder's trenches were filled with cinders, it was concluded that the brick piers were associated with turn-of-the-nineteenth-century activities, specifically the erection of Consumers' Gas coal and coke conveying machinery in

Concrete pad

Cinders

Charcoal, ash,
and coal cinders

Sterile subsoil

Brick pier · Builder's trench
for concrete footing

Figure 4.8. Brick pier in south wall of Trench 2, west of the concrete footing.

Area of stratigraphy similar to west wall · Brick pier · Layer 4 Cinders · Area of stratigraphy similar to east wall

Figure 4.9. Brick pier in north wall of Trench 2.

1901 (Consumers' Gas Company 1887–1940:1901). It is likely that the brick piers were constructed as bases and/or supports for the first set of conveyers and trestles crossing the courtyard. A short length of iron rebar protruded from the interior of the central brick pier, corroborating this interpretation.

Iron rebar

Brick pier

Limestone footing

Figure 4.10. Brick pier and cinders (right) and limestone footing overlaid by brick rubble (left), west of rail spur wall.

A number of courses of unmortared bricks were encountered in the south wall of the trench, immediately east of the concrete footing (Figure 4.1:#112; Figure 4.11). Moreover, a 75-centimetre-wide cut stone platform set in sterile subsoil was uncovered immediately below the bricks (Figure 4.1:#109). Fortunately, one of the bricks was impressed with "P.R.M. & M. CO. ST. LOUIS XXX" (Figure 4.12:a), while another had "P.R.M. & M. CO. NO.1."

With this information at hand, it was simply a matter of tracking down their origins. The bricks were examined by Chris Andreae, an industrial archaeologist who had prepared the history of the gas works presented in Chapter 2. He identified them as refractory bricks (a brick produced for use in high-temperature environments). These two brands of brick were manufactured in St. Louis between 1927 and 1930 (Gurcke 1987). Although the function of the stone and brick feature remains unknown, it clearly dated to the Consumers' Gas era.

The small area west of the concrete footing was excavated to a depth of 160 centimetres. Below the layer of cinders was a ten-centimetre layer of charcoal, ash, corroded metal, and cinders (Figure 4.1:#15), underlain by yellow clay sterile subsoil at a depth of 50 centimetres. Although no analyzable

Figure 4.11. Cut stone and 1920s brick exposed in the south wall of Trench 2.

artifacts were found and no dates were assigned to these stratigraphic layers, it is believed that they date to the Consumers' Gas era based on their composition. The subsoil was excavated to a depth of one metre west of the concrete footing to ensure that the excavation had, in fact, reached sterile, original clay.

The archival record of the Consumers' Gas era revealed that the large gas-manufacturing facility on the south side of Front Street was, even by today's

Figure 4.12. Brick impressed with P.R.M. & M. CO. ST. LOUIS XXX (a); brick with oval frog (b).

standards, an immense undertaking. Fortunately, the construction of the three principal buildings on the property occurred in the 1880s and not the 1980s. Whereas today the entire block would have been excavated to a great depth to accommodate development, one must remember that a century ago, the foundation for each and every building had to be dug by hand, using labourers, horses, and carts. It really isn't that surprising, then, that the archaeological exploration yielded evidence of only surface treatments, conveyor support piers, and a rail spur wall. What was surprising was what else was under the courtyard!

The Home District Gaol Era (1837–1887)

Somewhat surprisingly, the Home District Gaol was not well represented in the excavation trenches by either confirmed structural remains or features. While the large, broken limestone pieces in the area east of the rail spur may have been the remnants of the limestone blocks used in the construction of the gaol, the absence of any datable artifacts in association with these stones made their definitive identification difficult.

Evidence of the Home District Gaol was collected, however, from an area immediately adjacent to the rail spur wall on its west side. Underlying the cinders, which covered most of the site, was a narrow triangle of brown clay (Figure 4.1:#10), overlying a deep deposit of dark brown clay (Figure 4.1:#8) which was excavated to a depth of more than a metre (Figure 4.13). The dark brown clay contained a large quantity of stones, possibly river or lake cobbles, as well as pieces of granite. The stones dominated the excavation unit — in fact, there were more stones than soil. The dark brown soil was considered to be secondary fill, possibly related to the demolition of the Home District Gaol in the late 1880s, while the rocks may have represented the disturbed remains of a foundation wall.

Within the upper brown clay, 15 artifacts were found, including a broken piece of window glass, a brick fragment, nine animal bones, and four ceramic fragments — a single sherd each of creamware and whiteware, and two pieces of pearlware, all undecorated. This juncture in the excavation marked the first appearance of readily dateable ceramic wares. These wares generally consisted of fragments of either plates, bowls, cups, saucers, or other items found in dinner sets and table settings. Manufactured in England and imported to North America, ceramic wares are readily assigned to particular periods based on their dates of manufacture and availability.

One of the earliest imported wares in Upper Canada was creamware. Creamware is distinguished by a cream-coloured ceramic body over which a clear lead glaze was applied to let the colour of the body show through. The pooling of glaze, especially in footrings, leaves a distinctive green-yellow hue. The manufacture and popular use of creamware ceramics typically date from circa 1770 to 1820. Pearlware is also an early ware type and is identified by a nearly white-coloured body over which a blue or greyish tinted lead glaze was applied. The pooling of glaze leaves a distinctive blue hue on pearlware, whose period of manufacture and popular use date from circa 1780 to 1830.

Whitewares, on the other hand, have a dense, refined white earthenware

Figure 4.13. Excavation of Home District Gaol era deposits, west of rail spur wall.

body, somewhat harder than either creamware or pearlware. A clear lead glaze was applied over a variety of decorative techniques, such as sponging or hand-painting. The manufacture of whiteware ceramics typically dates from circa 1820 to the present day. Whiteware was most popular in the nineteenth century between, 1830 and 1860, until it was replaced by ironstone. Ironstone is a thick and heavy white to greyish-white ceramic, often called granite ware, typically with moulded relief decoration. The thick white lead glaze has a greyish or bluish tint. Manufactured as early as 1845, ironstone overtook whiteware in popularity during the 1860s. There are too few ceramic artifacts from the brown clay to reach a clear interpretation of either the origin of the clay or to characterize the assemblage, other than to say that the ceramics range in date from the early 1800s to the mid- to late nineteenth century.

There was also a layer of crushed brick, or brick rubble (Figure 4.1:#5), generally east of the concrete footing, below the cinders, at a depth of 50 centimetres below the surface. The brick was very poorly preserved, with few fragments larger than a quarter of a brick. The brick rubble had a thickness of approximately ten centimetres on the north side of the trench and thinned towards the south side, disappearing altogether along the southern wall of the excavation. The brick rubble was at the same depth and abutted the brown clay adjacent to the rail spur wall (Plate 7).

Within the crushed brick, towards the eastern edge, were partial bricks that could be assigned to two particular time periods. Occasionally, bricks have distinct characteristics that can help identify the period during which they were made. The dimensions of a brick increase slightly over time as their method of manufacture changes from hand to machine manufacture. Equally diagnostic are the impressions called frogs, the earliest of which were formed using hand-impressed moulds, while later frogs were formed during the process of mechanized manufacture. Along the east side of the brick rubble, a number of bricks were found which had hand-impressed oval frogs measuring 14 centimetres long (5 inches) by 7.5 centimetres (3 inches) wide (Figure 4.12:b). These bricks were older than the ones used to construct the brick piers, for not only were they smaller than the bricks used in the piers, but oval frogs date, in the Toronto area, to the late 1830s. They were not generally used after the mid- to late nineteenth century. Based on this information, the brick structure with which they were associated was likely constructed during the Gaol era.

Equally interesting was the appearance of a north-south linear feature of stones (Figure 4.1:#105) towards the eastern edge of the brick rubble, demarcating a boundary between the rubble and the brown clay (Figure 4.14). The partial bricks with oval frogs were found immediately above these stones. A question that remained to be answered was that if the brick rubble layer contained evidence of the destruction of a Gaol era building, then was the stone feature a structural remnant of this and/or an earlier building? This question could not be answered at this point in the excavation.

Removing the brick rubble revealed a layer of yellow clay (Figure 4.1#6), measuring between five and ten centimetres in thickness, which included some brick fragments. The clay was compact and dense and, upon excavation, literally peeled away from the underlying soil. The yellow clay was also found amongst the linear feature of stones, but did not extend east beyond the stones.

Below the yellow clay was a grey-brown soil (Figure 4.1:#7), located at a depth of 55 to 60 centimetres below the asphalt surface. This layer also extended to the edge of the stones but did not continue beyond them. There were numerous fragments of charcoal in the grey-brown soil, in addition to mortar and brick fragments.

Were these underlying deposits also related to the construction and occupation of the Home District Gaol? In response to this question, the focus of the excavation turned for the first time to the artifacts. Up to this point, only a meager collection of artifacts had been found. To the delight of all involved, the brick rubble layer contained an astonishing 968 artifacts, of which 765 were found directly above or immediately east of the linear stone feature. It is important to understand that with the law of superposition, the artifacts, by virtue of their inclusion in the brick rubble, had to originate from an activity

Figure 4.14. Andrew Clish mapping the linear stone feature.

period dating no earlier than the late 1830s. In other words, in order for the artifacts to be included in the brick rubble, they could not have been placed there prior to the building's occupation or destruction. They also had to have been discarded prior to the time at which the cinders were deposited.

An additional 210 artifacts were found in the yellow clay and a further 203 artifacts were recovered from the underlying grey-brown soil. In fact, once the entire excavation was complete, the artifacts from these three excavation layers accounted for more than half of the entire site collection. By grouping the brick rubble, the yellow clay, and the grey-brown soil artifacts together into one analytical unit, consisting of nearly 1,400 artifacts, the time period that these artifacts best represented was determined.

Far from glamorous, the artifacts included 297 pieces of window glass, which could be grouped into two categories based on their relative thickness. Window glass is of varying thickness, corresponding with the date of manufacture. It has been demonstrated that window glass thickness displays a trend towards stronger and thicker glass over the span of the nineteenth century (Kenyon 1980). Sites dating to earlier than circa 1850 typically have an average window glass thickness of less than 1.6 millimetres (or thin window glass) while those dating to post-1850 have a thickness greater than 1.6 millimetres (or thick window glass). Thick glass accounted for 154 of the glass fragments from the brick rubble, slightly favouring the post-1850 period.

The ceramic artifacts from the three layers represented a cross-section of ceramic types that included 36 creamware, 25 pearlware, 31 whiteware (Figures 4.15 and 4.16), and 6 ironstone sherds. This varied collection did not lend itself to any detailed analysis other than to conclude that activities causing these artifacts to be discarded spanned a lengthy period of time, possibly as early as the early 1800s and into the 1860s. The low frequency of ceramics, compared to the total number of artifacts recovered from the brick rubble, indicated that this deposit did not represent a domestic or household garbage dump such as one would find on a typical farm or urban household dating from the same time period. Rather, it was more representative of a deposit associated with a public building. Moreover, the presence of the early creamware and pearlware sherds in these deposits, mixed with later wares, suggested that an earlier structure or garbage area was nearby.

Adding to this uncharacteristic collection was the observation that the most frequent type of artifact found not only within the brick rubble, but also in each of the subsequent soil layers, was animal bone — 578 pieces in all. Stephen Cox Thomas, of Bioarchaeological Research, conducted an analysis of these and other bones from the site (Archaeological Services Inc. 2001). A sample of the animal bones from these layers resulted in the identification of 93 bones to species. Domestic specimens included 52 ox, 5 pig, 11 sheep, and 11 chicken; while wild species consisted of a small number of fish and snowshoe hares. In addition, these units were the only excavation levels to contain the remains of rats, accompanied by the presence of bones gnawed by rodents, implying that the bones were left exposed for some time before

Figure 4.15. Whiteware: mulberry floware rim sherd (a) and body sherd (b); blue transfer-printed (c); yellow slip (d); banded (e); glassy black slip (f).

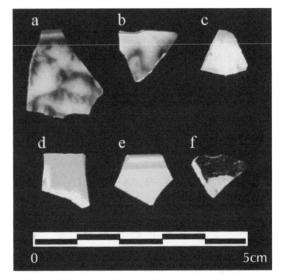

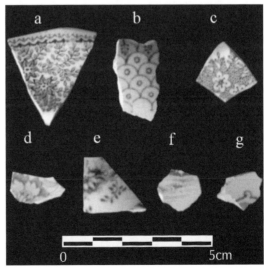

Figure 4.16. Whiteware: brown transfer-printed (a, c); blue transfer-printed (b, d-g).

being covered with earth or more refuse.

Curiously, the majority of the ox bone was derived from skulls, and of these, most were from the base of the skull, which is an exceedingly rare occurrence. The explanation offered by Thomas was that the remains suggested a bias, on the part of the site occupants, for ox heads. Moreover, an examination of the ox teeth concluded that most of the animals were at least five years in age, and many, if not most, may have been double that, well past the prime age for meat animals. With these results, even the upper class preference for calf's head during the nineteenth century cannot be used as a satisfactory explanation for the presence of this large quantity of aged ox skull bones. Moreover, Thomas suggested that the ox cranial material was generated on a large scale, perhaps as part of an inexpensive institutional diet, in which broth was a major component. Nineteenth century prison diets were typified by rations of soup and bread, supplemented by whatever the families of the inmates could provide. It seems safe to conclude, therefore, that these low status dietary remains are related to the Home District Gaol.

Artifacts of a more personal nature were also recovered within the three excavation units. A single coin, found in the eastern part of the brick rubble, was identified as a copper blacksmith token dating to circa 1835 (Figure 4.17 and Plate 8). Originating from Lower Canada, blacksmith tokens were designed as counterfeits of old English and Irish regal George III half-pennies. The dies were purposefully left unfinished, without dates or legends, and artificially darkened in order to give the appearance of an aged, badly worn coin. These coins were ultimately accepted in trade because of the lack of small change in Lower and Upper Canada at that time. The plain-edged token recovered from the site displayed, on the obverse, a Laureate bust of George III and, on the reverse, a tall, thin Britannia, seated right. The coin's design was copied from the English regal copper of 1770–1775 (Cross 1990:190, 192).

Figure 4.17. Copper blacksmith token dating to circa 1835, showing the obverse face bearing a Laureate bust of George III.

Decorated and undecorated smoking pipes were a common way to enjoy one's tobacco. Theses pipes were manufactured from white ball clay, and were mass-produced in both England and in Lower Canada. Because their designs are distinctive, the pipe bowls can be used as effective means of dating, aided by the common practice of stamping the manufacturer's name on the lengthy pipe stem. Of the 27 pipe fragments found in the three excavation layers in question, identifiable pipe bowls included two examples of a four-band fluted pipe, with band 3 (a ridged collar) and band 4 (wide, tapering ribs) visible. The four-band fluted style was manufactured by many companies, including the Montréal firms

Figure 4.18. TD-impressed pipe bowl recovered from the brick rubble. The top of the pipe is heavily charred.

of Bannerman and Henderson, in the post-1840 period (Kenyon 1982a). Impressed monograms bearing the letters "TD" were probably the most common pipe decoration and are frequently recovered from nineteenth century sites in Canada. The origin of this style of pipe dates back to 1755, when a British maker with these initials first impressed TD on a pipe bowl. This trademark was subsequently copied by any number of makers on both sides of the Atlantic. Decorated TD pipes were eventually replaced by plain or undecorated (save for an impressed TD on the bowl) pipes prior to the mid-nineteenth century (Kenyon 1982b, 1982c). Eight fragments of two pipe bowls comprising examples of TD-impressed border pipes, dating from 1825 to 1840, were found in the grey-brown soil. A single plain TD-impressed pipe bowl fragment, dating from the 1830s or 1840s, was found in the brick rubble (Figure 4.18).

The only clothing-related artifacts recovered were three buttons. A shell button (Plate 19:d) was recovered from the grey-brown soil. This polished four-hole, sew-through fastener button, measuring 10 millimetres in diameter with a plain flat front, was typically used on shirts and blouses. Shell (or pearl) buttons were most popular post-1820, although the date of introduction is unclear (Ferris 1986:100). The other buttons, made of bone, were polished, dish-shaped in cross-section, with concave fronts, and raised, rounded rims (Figure 4.19:b-c). Faint concentric striations on the back of these buttons suggest manufacture using a lathe. This type of bone button was very common and was used on everyday clothing items, such as outerwear or shirts, for a lengthy period spanning the first half of the nineteenth century.

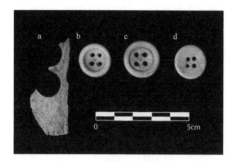

Figure 4.19. Bone button blank (a); bone buttons (b-d).

In addition, a broken fragment of a bone button blank, 50.5 millimetres long and 20 millimetres wide, was found (Figure 4.19:a). Two circular disks, each approximately 12.5 millimetres in diameter, had been cut out of a rib from a large animal, such as an ox.

In summary, the nearly 1,400 artifacts deposited in the brick rubble, the yellow clay, and the grey-brown soil appear to have originated, for the most part, with the mid-nineteenth century occupation of the property, as projected by the dates assigned to the recovered artifacts. It is possible that the blacksmith token was dropped by a labourer during the construction of the Home District Gaol. Likewise, the smoking pipes date to the same time period. The bone garbage may have been part of a dump from the gaol's kitchen, possibly just outside of the wall. Perhaps the button blank was the work of a jailed debtor, desperate to mend his last shirt. Simply, the artifacts from the three excavation levels indicate a strong relationship with the period of the construction and use of the Home District Gaol.

Despite the massive undertaking involved in the construction of the imposing limestone institution, the three small excavation trenches on the property did not reveal any clear significant structural remains attributed to the construction of the gaol, although the large limestone pieces documented east of the rail spur wall may well have been fragments of the large blocks used during its construction. The historic plan overlays confirm that the gaol was located to the immediate east of the projected footprint of the Parliament buildings and the middle excavation trench. Future excavations in that area may be successful in uncovering structural evidence of the large edifice and would perhaps enrich the present artifact assemblage.

During the excavation, however, it was the increasing presence of numerous early nineteenth century creamware and pearlware sherds in the lowest soil layers that captured the attention of the archaeologists. Their presence suggested that even earlier deposits underlying the Gaol era material remained to be explored.

The First and Second Parliament Buildings Era
(1797–1824)

The layer of brick rubble held the first clues in the search for Upper Canada's first and second Parliament buildings — these were the presence of a few creamware and pearlware sherds and fragments of early nineteenth century bricks. Indeed, two distinct types of brick were observed within the rubble: the ones that exhibited the hand-impressed oval frogs; and much smaller, plain ones. The smaller ones measured 20.5 by 10 by 5 centimetres (8 by 4 by 2 inches) in length, width, and height. Bricks in this size range were generally hand-made, do not have a frog, and were made in the early nineteenth century. Setting this archaeological clue in perspective, bricks recovered from excavations over the past few decades at Toronto's Fort York have these dimensions and characteristics, and date to circa 1800 (Figure 4.20). Even more intriguing was the fact that much of the identified early brick in the rubble displayed clear evidence of burning or charring on one of two faces of the brick fragment. When burned, brick will display not only a blackened face on the side directly exposed to the flames, but the heat of the fire also causes a chemical alteration during which the red clay fabric of the brick's interior takes on a greyish colour. These characteristics were noted on the early brick forms that were recovered from the site as traits that could only have been caused by the effects of post-manufacture burning.

In short, the archaeological evidence portrayed a brick rubble layer which contained bricks dating to between 1800 and 1830, as well as those dating to the late 1830s, or later. The presence of both brick types in the rubble pointed to a wall or structure that had been rebuilt on or close to its original location and then demolished at a later time, but before the cinders were deposited.

Figure 4.20. Fort York brick dating to circa 1800.

As word of the recovery of early nineteenth century materials spread through city and provincial offices, the media also began to take notice of the archaeological excavation occurring in that small parking lot off Front Street. From then on, local, national, and even international radio, newspapers, and television channels featured the Parliament buildings dig — and this was just the beginning of the discoveries (Plate 10).

In the northern section of the excavation trench, a layer of charcoal (Figure 4.1:#14) was encountered below the grey-brown soil, the layer which was attributed to the Home District Gaol period. The charcoal formed a thin but identifiable lens at varying depths in the excavation trench, ranging from 55 centimetres to 65 centimetres below the asphalt surface. Below the charcoal was a black, organic soil containing some small pieces of charcoal (Figure 4.1:#9). This soil was determined to be a buried topsoil layer, but it would have been the ground surface at some point in the past. One hundred artifacts were found within the organic soil, which extended across the northern and southern portions of the excavation trench, including 40 ceramic sherds, 41 animal bones (including ox, sheep, pig, and white-tailed deer), two smoking pipe fragments, four nails, and two pieces of window glass.

There were 22 creamware, 11 pearlware, and 5 whiteware sherds found in the organic topsoil layer. Only one of the creamware sherds had any decoration — creamwares in general were often undecorated. The yellow and brown decorated rim sherd was an example of one of the earliest hand-painted ceramics available in Upper Canada, referred to as early palette on creamware (Plate 12). This decoration, dating from circa 1780 to 1800, was also used on pearlware ceramics until the early 1830s. They typically depicted delicately painted leaves and foliage in soft or muted brown, yellow, orange, blue, and green colours, or simply in monochrome blue. Six of the pearlware sherds were decorated by means of a transfer print, a process that essentially mechanized and replaced the hand-painting of dinner services. Transfer prints were made on pearlware ceramics from circa 1800 to 1830. Typical of the early prints was the presence of a "soft" print (versus the hard, sharp edges of later transfer prints), first in blue, them in black. All of the pearlware transfer print artifacts were blue soft prints, often called "olde blue." Three of the whiteware ceramics were decorated: two with mulberry- coloured flow decoration, dating from circa 1845, while the other was an example of late palette hand-painted decoration, with red and green flowers and leaves, distinguished by a bolder use of colour than the early palette style. Late palette decorations were manufactured between 1830 and 1875. From 38 diagnostic ceramic sherds, all but three dated to before 1830, with the creamware being especially early, suggesting that a substantial deposit of early nineteenth century material was nearby.

A fascinating discovery was then made in the southern part of the excavation trench, at the interface between the organic topsoil and the sterile subsoil 60 centimetres below the surface. A set of linear charcoal stains (Figure 4.1:#112) was noted directly above the subsoil. These charcoal stains had a clear and distinct outline — they were the charred remains of partial lengths of two floorboards, running in a north-south direction (Figure 4.21). Two areas within the charred material indicated that the floorboards had burned completely through to subsoil, leaving no identifiable charcoal remains, but rather fire-reddened subsoil. This distinctive orange-red stained sand confirmed that an episode of intense heat occurred in this area, resulting in the creation of the ghostly images of the floorboards. The subsequent burial of these fragile soil stains by additional material, which must have occurred very soon after the fire, ensured their preservation. The only known fires in this area of the property were the one set by Americans during the War of 1812; and the 1824 chimney fire in the second Parliament buildings. The stains of the floorboards were not excavated, in order to preserve them for future archaeological examination. Already, the archaeological team had guessed that what they were finding would be of interest to Canadians for generations to come!

An equally exciting find was made a few metres to the north of the floorboards when the presence of additional linear charcoal stains was observed (Figure 4.1#111). Hand trowelling revealed that the stains were again at the interface between the organic topsoil and sterile subsoil, at a depth of 75 centimetres below the asphalt surface. A set of four linear stains extended east-west, parallel to each other (Figure 4.22). The fact that the charcoal stains were evenly spaced, of somewhat regular width, and extended to the linear feature of stones (found to the east of the stains) suggested that they represent four floor joists, or sleepers, that had burned *in situ*. Furthermore, the floor joists, as is typical in most floor construction, were perpendicular to the charred floorboards. Interestingly, similar evidence for sleepers being placed directly on subsoil was documented during excavations at Fort York — on buildings dating to the Parliament buildings era (Figure 4.23).

Two small, subsurface features were also present below the organic topsoil. One of the features, given its proximity to the fragile floorboards, was not investigated other than to document its location and surface composition. It

Figure 4.21. Charred remains of partial lengths of two floorboards in Trench 2, also showing the limestone footing, lime mortar, and cut stone.

measured 35 centimetres by 70 centimetres, with distinctly rounded corners (Feature 3; Figure 4.1:#119). It is not known if the feature was contemporary with or post-dated the floorboards. The second was a soil stain (Feature 1; Figure 4.1:#106) consisting of a 30 by 20 centimetre rectangular patch of clay, mottled with mortar, and brick fragments, located 77 centimetres below the asphalt surface. Upon excavation, Feature 1 proved to be a relatively shallow, flat-bottomed pit, cut into the sterile subsoil. The soil within the pit was brown to grey, sandy clay mottled with charcoal and red brick fragments. Three small pieces of limestone were located in the upper level of the feature, towards the edges of the pit. It is possible that both subsurface features are residual stains left from the placement of large wooden posts into the subsoil.

A small patch of mortar (Figure 4.1:#107) was noted on the subsoil in the centre of the excavation trench, at a depth of 80 centimetres below the asphalt surface. The patch was less than one centimetre thick and no artifacts were observed within the mortar, nor in the immediately surrounding subsoil. The mortar consisted of sand and lime, a type that was in use until the late nineteenth century. It was usually a mix of lime, sand, and water in a 2:1 ratio of lime to sand (McKee 1973). A larger deposit of the same lime mortar was found in the southern part of the trench at a similar depth. Here the lime

Figure 4.22. The charred remains of four floor joists in Trench 2.

Figure 4.23. Fort York pre-War of 1812 structure (Operation 1FY5) floor joists or sleepers. *(Courtesy of David Spittal)*

mortar extended for approximately 80 centimetres in a north-south orientation, although the more recent rail spur wall had disturbed its eastern edge. The lime mortar was left *in situ*.

The north-south linear feature of stones, to which the charred floorboards had been attached, was also thoroughly investigated. It was situated towards the eastern edge of the brick rubble and appeared initially at the level of the rubble continuing down to sterile subsoil (Plate 13). The stone was all of the same type — limestone consisting of very fine-grained, medium to dark grey pieces, containing occasional fossils. The distribution of the limestone was limited to a narrow 60-centimetre north-south line that was about 30 centimetres thick. The stones were relatively small, measuring between 5 and 20 centimetres in length, and were set into the sterile subsoil. There was no evidence of any mortar between the stones (Figure 4.24).

With this information in hand, the limestone feature was identified as the footing for a building. Footings serve two purposes: to act as a solid base upon which to build a foundation; and to function as a drain to draw water away from the structure. For either purpose, there would be no need to set the footing in mortar. As a drain feature, the footing is typically wider than the wall, extending away from the structure. For this purpose, a foot-

Figure 4.24. Detail of unmortared limestone footing in Trench 2.

ing is typically laid in a trench directly within subsoil. A yellow clay-filled builder's trench was clearly observed adjacent to the limestone footing. The lack of larger cut fieldstone, and the presence of a considerable quantity of brick in the upper level of the footing, indicates either that the structures with which the footing was associated were constructed directly on the stone footing or that the fieldstone had been removed at some later date. That the limestone had been laid directly in the yellow subsoil clay implied that the limestone footing was constructed as a dry-laid footing, using clay as the binding agent.

At this point, the archaeological team began to wonder if the limestone footing, in association with the charred floor joists and floorboards, might represent the east wall of a structure. Using the historic plan overlays, it was determined that the limestone footing could easily be the east wall of one of the south buildings of the first Parliament buildings. It is also likely that the limestone footing was reused and/or expanded upon during the period of gaol construction, circa 1838–1840, given the presence of complete and fragmented bricks with hand-pressed oval frogs in the upper levels of the limestone footing.

Archaeological investigations at Fort York have revealed the use of loose siltstone footings for the Lieutenant Governor's House. These footings were constructed in the same manner as the limestone footing at the Front Street excavation, consisting of a 60-centimetre (two-foot) wide dry-laid footing, lined with clay, at an approximate depth of 30 centimetres (one foot) below the former ground surface (Figure 4.25).

The limestone itself was identified as Gull River limestone by Peter von

Bitter and David Rudkin of the Royal Ontario Museum, as well as by Derek Armstrong of the Ontario Geological Survey, and by Ed Freeman, a geological consultant. According to von Bitter, although Gull River limestone outcrops throughout Ontario, from Manitoulin Island to the Kingston area, the most likely source of this material at the end of the eighteenth century would have been Kingston. A thriving town at this time (in contrast to York), Kingston already had a well-established quarrying industry. Many, or most, of the contemporary and later stone buildings there were built of fine-grained Gull River limestone.

Figure 4.25. Collapsed unmortared stone foundation wall of the Lieutenant Governor's house at Fort York, circa 1800. *(Courtesy of David Spittal)*

Shipment of this material to Toronto by the well-established Lake Ontario transport system also seems more likely, given the state of roads at the time. Moreover, if the exposed footing was part of those of the Parliament buildings, these would have been constructed by the military, and it seems sensible that they would order, where possible, construction materials from their own sources, such as the quarries at Kingston. Even a few decades later, the limestone rock bed visible at the Lake Ontario beach was deemed too expensive for quarrying. Indeed, it was noted on Bonnycastle's 1833 plan that, "Building stone of fine quality is therefore only to be had from Kingston, from Queenston, or from Hamilton on Burlington Bay."

The shape and uniform size of most of the limestone from the footing suggests to von Bitter that it may have been a byproduct of stonemasons and quarrymen shaping larger, more quadrate limestone blocks, particularly for use in the above-ground portion of stone structures. Rather than waste such a byproduct, the quarry operators may have saved and sold this material for use in foundations, much as crushed gravel is used today. On the other hand, it is possible that it was transported as blocks rather than broken stone. Indeed, the presence of limestone shatter within the limestone footing may indicate that the rock was broken on site. Limestone of this nature is broken by direct percussion, using hammers or mallets, which leaves distinct scars on the surfaces that are struck. Such scarring was observed on a number of the limestone specimens collected from the footing. In sum, detailed consideration of the form of the limestone footing, its method of construction, and the source of the building material indicate a late eighteenth century date for its construction.

Thus, while the excavations had provided considerable evidence of the discovery of the Parliament buildings — in the form of an original topsoil containing small quantities of early nineteenth century ceramics; charred circa 1800 bricks, *in situ* burned floorboards and joists, and a limestone footing dating in construction style and materials to the early 1800s — the proverbial smoking gun was still missing. What was needed were artifacts that could *directly* associate these features with the 1797 to 1824 period. A complex feature of mortar, charcoal, and stone, which came to be known simply as Feature 2, provided just such a key piece of evidence.

A small patch of charcoal found in the northwestern corner of the excavation trench lay overtop another patch of mortar (Figure 4.1:#116). This patch marked the beginning of Feature 2 (Figure 4.26), which in the end extended over a six-metre-square area west of the limestone footing, and was composed of a combination of large quantities of charcoal mixed with silty and granular black loam (Figure 4.1:#121), patches of lime mortar, and numerous flat siltstone rocks measuring between 10 and 20 centimetres in length (Figure 4.1:#117). The boundary of Feature 2 was defined to the east by the yellow clay comprising the builder's trench for the limestone footing, and to the south by the floor joists set in the subsoil. To the north and west, the feature extended beyond the limits of the excavation area (Figure 4.27).

In standard archaeological fashion, the feature was sectioned, in this case, in a north-south 50-centimetre-wide trench to establish both horizontal and vertical context between the feature and the surrounding soils. In the centre of the trench, at a depth of two to three centimetres below the surface level of Feature 2, was an extensive charcoal layer mottled with lime. Below this was an actual layer of siltstone rocks, which had been placed on organic topsoil mottled with charcoal fragments, followed by sterile subsoil (Plate 14).

The rock consisted of flaggy weathered (i.e., weathering in flat sheets), medium-grey to tan-coloured calcareous siltstone, which lacked fossils. This siltstone is of the locally occurring Georgian Bay Formation that underlies much of Toronto (Westgate and von Bitter 1999). This formation outcrops

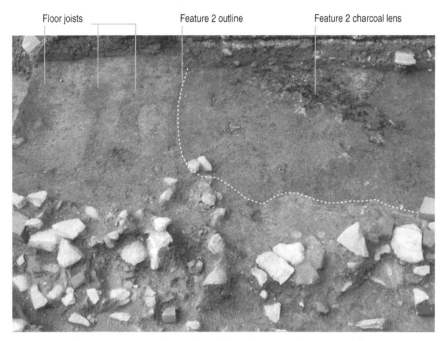

Figure 4.26. Feature 2 outline, charcoal lens, limestone footing, and floor joists.

naturally in many of the small creeks and rivers that flow south, through the Toronto region, into Lake Ontario. In the early 1800s, the material very likely would have been available in some of the creeks, such as the nearby Taddle Creek, or Garrison Creek in the vicinity of Fort York, or as eroded slabs on the beaches of Lake Ontario.

Given the emerging complexity in the character of Feature 2, the decision was made to carry out further investigation of the feature in one-metre units for context and control. The removal of the silty black loam, which was the predominant soil matrix in the feature, revealed more of the lime mortar patch, extending into the western wall of the excavation trench. Directly below the mortar layer, the thin, level layer of siltstone rocks was again documented. Mixed in with the siltstone rocks were numerous very small fragments of thin red brick, some of which were burned. In addition, to the north of this large patch of lime mortar and siltstones, a ten-centimetre deep linear ditch extended east-west from the west wall of the excavation to the east. The ditch would appear to have functioned as a sub-floor drain (Figure 4.1:#118), measuring 30 centimetres in width. The soil within the drain consisted of

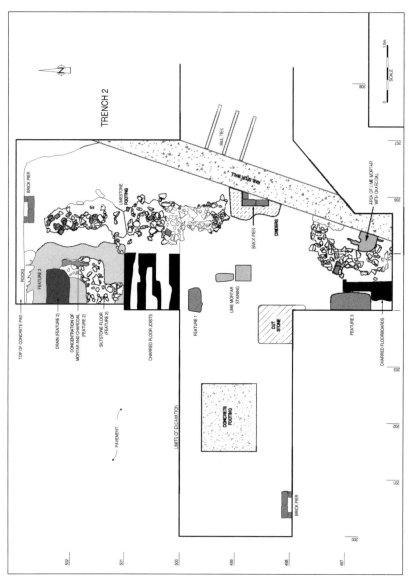

Figure 4.27. Feature 2 in relation to the excavation area in Trench 2.

mottled yellow clay mixed with charcoal and small stones. To the north of the drain, the silty black loam overlying the stone layer continued into the northern and western walls of the excavation trench.

No further excavation of the elements within Feature 2 was conducted, given that the feature extended well beyond the walls of the excavation. More importantly, however, the implications of the assemblage of artifacts found within the feature were quite clear. They pointed to the fact that the floor must have been associated with the first Parliament buildings. Having discovered the feature, it was incumbent upon the archaeological team to leave most of the exposed portion of the feature for future archaeological investigation, when a larger area could be explored.

Eight hundred and twenty-six artifacts were recovered from the excavation of Feature 2. What was remarkable was the overwhelming predominance of early nineteenth century materials. Of the 147 ceramic artifacts, 101 sherds were creamware, an additional 20 sherds were pearlware, and 2 were whiteware. There was also a single example of stoneware and 23 unidentifiable pieces of ceramic. In total, 98 percent of the identifiable ceramics from Feature 2 consisted of ceramic sherds dating to the 1780 to 1820 period. Among the remainder of the artifacts recovered were 44 fragments of window glass, 100 faunal specimens including a piece of shell, 3 smoking pipe fragments, and 88 nails.

All but two of the 101 creamware sherds from Feature 2 were plain or undecorated, but the sample included five broken rim fragments and three base fragments. The remainder consisted of body sherds. Fortunately, the rim sherds were large enough to identify the dinner service pattern as "Royal" (Figure 4.28). The manufacture of the Royal pattern spanned the 1780 to 1815 period. Royal, a similar pattern known as "New Queen's," together with a plain rim pattern known as "Paris" or "Plain," were the most common patterns in the circa 1780–1800 period (Sussman 1978). Indeed, the Royal creamware pattern has been recovered from Fort York in midden (garbage) deposits thought to be associated with the Government House, which was built as the Lieutenant Governor's residence and office in 1800, and was burned by the Americans during their occupation of the fort in 1813 (Spittal 1996:67).

A single example of inlaid slipped design was found on a creamware body fragment (Plate 15). The manufacture of such British ceramics dates from the 1790s to the 1820s. Inlaid slip decoration was made by cutting a pattern into the ceramic body after it was dipped, typically in dark brown slip (see

Figure 4.28. "Royal" pattern creamware: Fort York (left) and four rim sherds from Feature 2, Parliament buildings site (right).

Sussman 1997). This single sherd from Feature 2 represents an early example of inlaid brown slipped creamware, dating to circa 1795. A second decorated creamware sherd from Feature 2 was an orange slip-banded sherd. The remainder of the creamware was too fragmented to further any interpretations based on patterns or decoration.

The pearlware ceramics were decorated with common patterns of the time. Two pearlware sherds, decorated in hand-painted monochrome blue, were found in Feature 2 (Plate 16), as were two black transfer-printed sherds, displaying soft print characteristics dating to the 1820s. Two mended rim sherds from Feature 2 displayed a single wide brown band and a green rouletted rim design (Plate 15). Banded decoration on pearlware ceramics dates from 1780 to 1820 and was usually applied to bowls, pitchers, and mugs rather than dinner service or tea sets (Sussman 1997:9). Two plain or undecorated pearlware rim sherds were also found.

The three whiteware sherds from Feature 2 included a dark blue transfer print. Although no identifiable pattern was discernable from the small fragment found, it likely dates to between circa 1820 and 1830. Dark blue was the sole colour for early transfer-printed whitewares, while a lighter blue, as well as brown and black coloured prints were manufactured in the post-1830 period. A blue-edged whiteware rim sherd, with a scalloped impressed edge, was found in Feature 2. Although edged decoration was mass-produced between 1780 and 1840, the mean date of manufacture can be assigned to circa 1813 to 1834, based on the ware type in combination with the edge moulding style (Miller 1989).

Numerous varieties of stoneware ceramics were manufactured during the eighteenth and nineteenth centuries from British and local sources, making stoneware difficult to date with any degree of precision. The earliest stoneware manufacturer in York County was established by 1798 and the pottery operated for 50 years (Newlands 1979). The lone stoneware sherd from Feature 2 was very fine-grained and medium grey in colour, with a clear glaze on the exterior. Although British stoneware from circa 1800 was frequently salt-glazed, this sherd was not glazed in this manner. The Feature 2 sherd represented a finer piece of stoneware than would typically be available in Upper Canada and was identified by Dena Doroszenko, an historic archaeologist with the Ontario Heritage Foundation, as late eighteenth century in origin, likely from a British manufacturer (Plate 15).

Other artifacts from Feature 2 included window glass and nails. Thin window glass, typically dating to pre-1850s, comprised 98 percent of the glass fragments recovered. In comparison, in the layers above Feature 2 thick and thin window glass were represented almost equally, albeit with lesser frequencies. Hand-wrought nails, square in cross-section with a four-sided pyramidal head, typically dating from the late 1790s to 1830, accounted for 95 percent of the identified nails from Feature 2 (Plate 15).

There were also 99 animal bones found in Feature 2, and a single shell. Identified species among these remains included ox, pig, sheep, horse, and Canada goose. Two important findings emerged from Thomas' analysis of the bone from Feature 2 — one based on butchering techniques and the other on diet. The cleaver (and axe) and the bone saw were the two most common methods used by butchers to cut meat bones. Each tool left unique marks on the bone, used by analysts to assign general dates to artifacts with these marks. According to Thomas, during the early part of the nineteenth century, the cut surfaces of bones tend to have a rippled appearance and the cut was frequently completed by snapping the bone rather than finishing the cut. After the mid-nineteenth century, bone saw cuts tended to have smoother, more even surfaces and were cut clean through. In addition, meat cuts over the course of the nineteenth century changed from large, roast-sized cuts to the smaller and thinner individual steaks and chops, that remain the norm today.

From the eighteen cuts found in Feature 2, the 4:5 ratio of cleaver to saw cuts suggests an early nineteenth century date, as does the presence of three rippled saw cut surfaces, and the absence of thin cut bones. Moreover, many bones showed evidence of incomplete cuts, resulting in snapped edges. This evidence points to an early nineteenth century origin for these animal remains. In an urban setting, one would expect the presence of butcher shops soon after settlement occurred. By 1830–1831, for instance, there were three dozen butchers' stalls in the York market, leading to the assumption that most town residents were purchasing their meat rather than raising and butchering their own livestock. This, in turn, would suggest that by 1830 most cuts would not be characterized by cleaver marks or rippled cut surfaces. Their presence on the Feature 2 bones suggests an earlier date of deposition.

The recovered species and type of meat cuts also suggest an early date for the feature. Foremost, the use of wild game in the diet has been shown to decline over the course of the early to mid-nineteenth century (Jurney 1978:33, Thomas 1987:10). Feature 2, and the layer immediately above the feature, yielded the bones of Canada goose, passenger pigeon, and white-tailed deer.

For domestic animals, there was a tendency for pork to be less expensive than lamb and mutton, while certain beef cuts were the most expensive. The ratio of sheep to pig elements of approximately 3:1 reflects a consumer choice in favour of lamb or mutton rather than pork, which would have cost less. The eight identified beef bones represent meat cuts which are among the most expensive in today's market: short loin, sirloin, and rib roast (LeeDecker et al. 1987:246). Thomas concluded that the apparent emphasis on more highly valued beef cuts likewise reflects consumer choice and hints at a certain degree of affluence behind the choice. While it is not certain in what context the expensive cuts found on the site might have been used, their recovery, along with the wild game, suggests a quite different and much earlier diet than the other deposits of animal bone from the site.

As an assemblage, the artifacts recovered from Feature 2 can only have had an early nineteenth century origin. The predominance of burned thin brick, hand-wrought nails, and thin window glass can only relate to the construction of structure(s) between circa 1790 and 1840; while the overwhelming presence of creamwares, dating between 1780 and 1820 from within the feature, precludes it from dating to any period other than the parliamentary-era. For the archaeological team, Feature 2 was that elusive smoking gun.

It still remained, however, to interpret the feature. Based on the structural elements, it seemed clear that it was a portion of a prepared sub-floor, which extended into the northern and western walls of the excavation. It consisted of siltstone rocks overlain with lime mortar functioning as support for a wooden floor. The presence of burned floor joists to the south of the feature supported this interpretation. The drain likely precluded the use of wooden joists in this vicinity, requiring the use of mortared stone to raise the floor. Given that the burned floor joists extended to the limestone footing, the entire area west of the footing likely represented an original floor to a structure. While the first structure in this location may have been associated with the first Parliament buildings of Upper Canada, given the artifact assemblage in Feature 2, there is no evidence to preclude the use of the same floor in the reconstruction of the first buildings or in the second Parliament buildings complex.

There was more evidence, however, that the floor was initially associated with the first Parliament buildings. Small, ten-centimetre wide cross-sections of the floorboard and floor joist charcoal and sterile subsoil were taken for macro (seed) and micro (pollen) floral analyses. The results of this analysis, conducted by Stephen Monckton, of Bioarchaeological Research, were astounding (Archaeological Services Inc. 2001). The floor board and floor joist samples identified maple, beech, and red oak, with white pine from the charcoal layer immediately above. These were likely the woods used in either the construction of the buildings or in their furnishings.

The pollen analysis yielded even better results, with the identification of birch and white pine as the most common taxa found (Figure 4.29). Comparatively rare were oak, hickory, willow, and ironwood. Weeds such as chenopod, plantain, grass, and ragweed were also recorded, indicating the remains of a natural seed bank which would have existed in the soil prior to the construction of the building. Monckton concluded that these findings pointed to a picture of successional forest and weeds. He also noted, however, that while there is evidence of such a forest in the recovered data, the extremely low ragweed frequencies were consistent with a time of comparatively little forest clearance, such as the late eighteenth century in York. Indeed, the

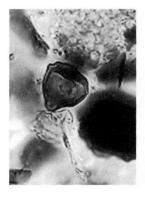 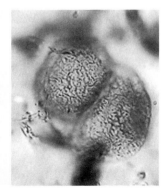

Figure 4.29. Left: birch pollen (*Betula papyrifera*); right: white pine pollen (*Pinus strobus*) (750x magnification).

sudden deforestation of southern Ontario during the middle of the nineteenth century is marked clearly on regional pollen diagrams by the sudden rise in the frequency of ragweed pollen.

Both the seeds and pollen would have been preserved by anaerobic conditions below the building floor. A number of seeds were charred. These were likely exposed to fire when the structure burned in 1813. It is likely that the subsequent renovations after the fire protected this botanical record. The later covering of the area with concrete and asphalt continued to protect the assemblage.

Indeed, the various construction activities that have occurred on the site played an essential role in the preservation of the archaeological record. On all archaeological sites, despite the law of superposition, some later materials, especially small fragments, inevitably find their way through natural and/or cultural processes, such as root or rodent action or construction disturbance, into earlier deposits. To counter this effect, archaeologists have to rely upon the relative frequencies of these artifacts to identify the age of deposits. For the period dating from 1795 to 1830, the principal activity area with respect to ceramic deposition was almost exclusively west of the limestone footing. Almost all of the creamware and pearlware ceramics were found west of the limestone footing, in direct association with the parliamentary-era floor; while east of the limestone footing, the number of these sherds dropped dramatically. The whiteware ceramics displayed quite a different pattern. The majority were found directly above the limestone footing in the brick rubble, reflecting a period of time contemporary with the Gaol era, after the building walls had been demolished, providing an opportunity for recently discarded artifacts to mix with the brick rubble and fall amongst the footing stones. The recovery of ironstone ceramics was confined to the northeastern portion of the excavation trench, east of the limestone footing and adjacent to the rail spur wall, and was therefore also associated with activities at the Home District Gaol. That no ironstone was recovered west of the limestone footing demonstrated that this area was effectively sealed prior to 1865, the date of introduction of this type of ceramic ware. It should be remembered that Feature 2 had already been sealed by the reconstruction of the first building and/or the construction of the second Parliament buildings.

Mindful of these findings, the archaeological team also went out of their way to contribute to the sealing and protection of previous deposits, especially those relating to the parliamentary era. After all mapping and photography in the three test trenches had been completed, and all the artifacts were recovered,

Figure 4.30. The backfilling of Trench 2 which involved laying down geotextile with plastic sheeting and clean sand fill to protect the fragile archaeological deposits.

each test trench was backfilled by machine up to the level of the asphalt, lightly packed, and re-surfaced. In order to preserve the *in situ* features and protect the fragile charcoal stained floorboard and joist features, however, a layer of clean sand was first placed over them, followed by geotextile and plastic sheeting, and a minimum of ten centimetres of clean sand fill was placed over the entire excavation area (Figure 4.30). The remainder of the fill comprised the loose soils from the excavation, while the larger concrete, asphalt, and rock materials were removed from the site. With these actions, the site is ready for further exploration in the future, when officials have decided the ultimate fate of these rare and fragile remains.

5

LESSONS FROM THE PAST

The archaeological test excavations at the Parliament site resulted in the discovery of incontrovertible evidence of the survival of archaeological deposits associated with the first and second Parliament buildings of Upper Canada. This evidence was amassed through systematic research involving a variety of investigative techniques and analyses. These included historic documentation and archival research, artifact identification and distributional analyses, stratigraphic and sub-surface archaeological feature interpretation, identification of historic construction techniques, as well as lithographic, botanical, and faunal analyses. Each analysis reached independent conclusions which collectively contribute to a compelling argument for the presence of parliamentary-era cultural remains. Given that in the late eighteenth through late nineteenth centuries the land was government-owned, thereby precluding significant residential use by others, the conclusion that the structural remains represent part of the parliamentary complex is inescapable. This section summarizes the collected evidence and then explores the municipal and provincial planning and management context for the conservation and interpretation of the site.

Archival Evidence

A number of historic plans and maps place the location of the first Parliament buildings on the lakefront of Lake Ontario, immediately west of the Taddle Creek outlet, in a government reserve area south of what is now Front Street and east of Berkley Street. Built between 1795 and 1797, the first Parliament complex included two brick buildings, facing west, which measured 40 feet by 24 feet. The structures were situated 75 feet apart from one another, but were joined by a covered colonade. The House of Legislative Council sat in the southern building and the House of Legislature Assembly in the northern building. The buildings were likely each one and a half storeys, with a small viewing gallery. To the immediate east of the brick buildings were two 30-foot-long frame structures used for committee rooms. These frame structures were connected to the brick buildings by means of a covered wooden platform. The inaugural session in Upper Canada's first Parliament buildings sat in June 1797. These buildings were destroyed in the spring of 1813 by American forces, but were rebuilt quickly as two-storey structures to house British troops. After the soldiers returned to Fort York, the upper floors were used as lodgings for new immigrants.

The second Parliament buildings complex was constructed beginning in 1819. The decision was made to construct a centre building between what remained of the rebuilt brick structures of the first Parliament complex, effectively filling in the 75-foot gap between the two wings, as had been proposed in the original design. The first session in the new second Parliament buildings, the eighth Parliament at York, sat in December 1820. The fate of the second Parliament buildings was similar to that of the first. In December of 1824, a fire broke out in the north wing — likely the result of sparks from an overheated chimney flue — and quickly spread to the main body of the building. The south wing was saved from complete destruction, although it suffered serious damage.

Although briefly occupied by Samuel Chearnley in 1827, the second Parliament buildings remained largely derelict until March 1830, when their fate was sealed by the decision that the remaining materials from the shell of the old buildings be sold by public auction. It was noted that not only were the walls falling to ruin, but that many of the bricks and stone had been removed already from the site. The property remained vacant until construction of the Home District Gaol began in 1838.

Four reliable archival maps, which depict the Parliament buildings, were overlain and an envelope developed which encompassed all of the depicted Parliament buildings. This envelope, therefore, represents the maximum area of highest potential for recovering parliamentary-era cultural remains. Most of Trench 2, which yielded the relevant archaeological remains, was indeed situated within this envelope. Moreover, the location of the parliamentary-era floor correlates perfectly with the documented location of a comparatively undeveloped area within the later District Gaol and Consumers' Gas complexes, as evident in the archival record.

Structural Evidence

Evidence pertaining to the presence of a structure on the property dating from circa 1800 was recovered in the form of fragmented early clay bricks above a dry laid limestone footing, the charred remains of wooden floor joists and floorboards, and Feature 2 consisting of large patches of lime-sand mortar and a flat siltstone subfloor. Based on the historic map overlays, it is possible that the Trench 2 excavation, within which these features were situated, was positioned on the east wall of the southern building of the first Parliament buildings.

The footing consisted solely of Gull River formation limestone, which was actively quarried at Kingston by the 1790s. The fact that limestone, rather than locally available siltstone, was used for the footings suggests that it was readily available through an established military supply system. That superior construction materials were employed in the project is supported by the observation that the first Parliament buildings were the first brick structures in York, as was befitting of their importance and stature.

Construction of the Parliament buildings footings appears to have followed similar methods to those employed at the garrison of Fort York a few years earlier, consistent with the fact that military personnel were involved in their construction. Archaeological investigations at the fort have documented the presence of loose siltstone footings for the officer's mess and the barracks, which were constructed in the same manner as the limestone footing at the Parliament site — a 60-centimetre (two-foot) wide dry-laid footing, lined with clay, at an approximate depth of 30-centimetres (one-foot). This style of footing was typical of late eighteenth and early nineteenth century construction methods, and visually, the techniques of footing construction documented at the Parliament site and at Fort York are virtually indistinguishable. Later nineteenth century footings are often mortared and accompanied by trimmed field stone foundations. It would appear that the first buildings were constructed directly on the limestone footings. It is also likely that later structures were erected using the same footings.

The presence of charred floor joists and floorboards overlying fire-reddened subsoil was documented here and in Simcoe-era structures at Fort York. At the Parliament site, the botanical analysis yielded evidence of an indigenous seedbank (including bramble, chenopod, and elderberry) and a prevalence of birch and pine pollen, within the soil under the charred boards and joists. These seeds represent colonizing species that would have grown quickly in an area that had been cleared for approximately six months. Normally, this botanical material would not have survived for any length of time, but both seeds and pollen would have been preserved by anaerobic conditions such as those found below a building floor. Moreover, the extremely low ragweed frequencies in the samples are consistent with an early nineteenth century date for the deposits, as this was a time of comparatively little forest clearance. A lack of pollen contamination from later, more prevalent species indicates that this assemblage is derived from a sealed deposit. Given the presence of charred floor boards and the fact that a number of the early brick fragments were burned, at least some charring of this seedbank might be expected to have occurred. Indeed, a small number of the seeds were charred, indicating that this original deposit dates from the short period between the clearing of the land, the construction of the first buildings, and the brief period of exposure after the 1813 fire before new flooring again sealed the deposit.

Artifactual Evidence

The artifact assemblage from Feature 2 and the layers associated with the structural features is consistent with the parliamentary era. Feature 2 is overwhelmingly dominated by creamware ceramics, manufactured in the late eighteenth and early nineteenth centuries. Datable creamwares included a fragment of inlaid slip decoration, circa 1795, and pieces attributed to the Royal pattern, circa 1790–1810, a pattern also recovered from 1990s excavations at the Fort York garrison. Moreover, the creamwares and pearlwares were located to the west of the limestone footing, thought to be the interior of the Parliament building. The later whitewares were observed to be situated amongst the upper levels of the limestone footings. These wares date to the circa 1830–1838 period, after the 1830 sale and removal of any remaining brick when the footings of the south wing of the Parliament buildings would have been exposed for the first time since 1813. The recovery of oval, frogged bricks from these same upper layers indicates that the footings were re-used during the Gaol era.

Thin window glass and hand-wrought nails within Feature 2 and the lower strata also provide clear evidence of the early date of those deposits. The presence of thicker window glass and machine-cut nails in the higher strata is consistent with the early nineteenth century lower layers having been sealed, as is also indicated by the results of the botanical analysis.

Finally, the cut mark evidence on the recovered faunal material suggests an early nineteenth century deposition. Butchering evidence, in the form of a higher ratio of cleaver to saw cuts, and the incidence of attributes associated with the early phase of saw use, was consistent with an early date. Additionally, the number and ubiquity of wild food resource remains also suggests a relatively early nineteenth century date, as does the lack of thin-cut bone sections more common in the latter half of the nineteenth century. On the other hand, the emphasis on cranial elements among the cattle component suggests an inexpensive institutional diet that was most likely associated with food preparation and refuse disposal during the early Gaol era. The vast majority of this later material was recovered to the east and outside of the early nineteenth century structural remains.

Together, the historical and archaeological data indicate that the excavation of Trench 2 revealed a small portion of the south wing of the first Parliament buildings complex. Moreover, the strata evident in the west and north walls of the excavation suggest that more of this burned floor remains intact under the paved surface.

Conservation and Interpretation: Whose Responsibility Is It?

In light of the conclusive identification of the early nineteenth century remains as those of Upper Canada's first and second Parliament buildings, the site is one of local, provincial, and national significance. Given the objectives of the 2000 United States National Parks Service *Revolutionary War and War of 1812 Historic Preservation Study,* the Parliament site is also of international significance as a key site from the War of 1812. It should be recognized as such by both Canada and the United States. Clearly, the site should be secured and interpreted to the public at large.

In June of 2001, the new *Heritage Toronto* released a report entitled *Observations on the State of Heritage,* representing the first time that an arms-length agency of the City of Toronto has prepared an overview of heritage management in the city. The report summarizes the issues facing the heritage conservation movement, both professional and volunteer, and for both below- and above-ground heritage, and provides a list of recommendations for immediate action. First among the priorities identified in this document is the need for co-ordination of heritage conservation efforts between the federal, provincial, and municipal levels. It is difficult to imagine an archaeological feature that is more deserving of a co-ordinated heritage conservation effort than the remains of the first Parliament buildings of Upper Canada. The deposits are on private land, subject to both municipal and provincial planning legislation, and are of local, provincial, national, and even international significance. It is not surprising then that the various levels of government are considering carefully how to define their roles in the permanent conservation of these rare and fragile remains.

While the Toronto City Council had passed a bylaw to designate the property under the Ontario Heritage Act in 1997, because it was known that the first Parliament buildings had existed on the block, it had always been assumed that institutional and industrial development would have destroyed any archaeological deposits. To the credit of the City's Culture Division, however, they arranged for access and funding with the landowners to undertake an archaeological investigation of the property. They did so despite professional opinions that it was very unlikely that anything related to the parliamentary era would have survived. It is indeed fortunate that the Culture Division, which is charged with the responsibility for the preservation of the City's heritage, pursued the matter. The Culture Division will also continue to safeguard the site through the administration of both municipal and provincial planning policies. In fact, Ontario's Planning Act is quite clear that municipalities should ensure, for any project requiring planning approval, that potential impacts to archaeological features are fully mitigated. By definition, mitigation may entail either protection or salvage excavation.

Defining which is the appropriate option in this case is the province's responsibility. As manager of provincial heritage resources, as defined in the Planning Act, it makes the decision. Furthermore, the fact is that the small brick buildings were constructed for the sitting of the Parliament of Upper Canada, which is present-day Ontario. While there are certainly municipal and federal interests in the remains, it is the Province of Ontario that bears the largest and most legitimate responsibility to act in the current situation.

In light of the national and international significance of the site, however, the federal government should assign the site national historic designation, and should aid the Province in the acquisition of the site. There is a considerable amount of land in the vicinity of the site that is already owned by the Province.

Destruction of the archaeological remains, as would occur should they be salvage excavated completely, is not an appropriate action in this case. While some excavation might be necessary for the purposes of on-site interpretation, a foundation of the archaeological paradigm is the preservation of significant archaeological sites, either in part or in their entirety, to allow for future generations to revisit and re-interpret the remains, possibly using yet-to-be discovered techniques and methods of analysis. It would be equally irresponsible, however, to attempt to interpret the site anywhere other than its original location. Many have argued, quite correctly, that this location should be secured and the history of the Parliament buildings interpreted there, regardless of the presence of physical remains. There is a sense of place, in this most significant setting, that can not be defined by the presence or absence of archaeological remains.

The need for interpretation is inescapable. Should one wish to introduce a visitor to Toronto to its late eighteenth or early nineteenth century colonial history, there are only a few options, including Fort Rouillé (identified only by a plaque), Fort York, or a trip to the Canadian history section in a local library. While Fort York and other military establishments represent an essential component in the presentation and understanding of the genesis and development of Toronto and Ontario, alone they present both a singular and narrow perspective. Given the importance that our first legislative buildings had to the people of the day — they referred to them as the Palaces of Government — is it not imperative that we tell their story on the very site where these palaces stood?

Given the context of overlapping and confusing jurisdictional responsibilities for this site, it is interesting and not at all unusual that the impetus for the archaeological exploration came from a local heritage advocacy group — The Citizens for the Old Town. They were instrumental in encouraging the City to explore the archaeological potential of the site and along with other heritage groups have played comparable roles for numerous projects related to the conservation and interpretation of the Old Town. There is a very clear role for the public in heritage conservation, and Toronto is blessed with an active and informed community that will continue not only in the management of heritage features, but also to guide this work.

In that regard, the award-winning pamphlet, prepared by The Citizens for the Old Town, entitled *You Can Often See the Vision of a City by How It Views Its Past*, provides counsel to all levels of government on what can be achieved in this situation. The pamphlet applauds the preservation and interpretation of sites, such as Benjamin Franklin's House in Philadelphia; Pointe-à-Callière, an archaeological site and museum that celebrates the birthplace of Montréal; and the site of the first government house in Sydney, Australia, juxtaposing these fitting interpretations with the image of a car wash on the site of Upper Canada's first Parliament buildings.

There are larger lessons stemming from the discovery of archaeological remains of the Parliament buildings. In October 2000, faced with an understanding of the current-day commercial and former institutional and industrial uses of the property, there was little hope among the archaeological team members of finding even a trace of the first Parliament buildings. The discovery of *in situ* evidence of the 1 May 1813 burning of the first Parliament buildings by American forces, in an attack on York during the War of 1812, surprised elected and representative officials, the citizens of Toronto and Ontario, and the archaeologists themselves. The lesson is that the City's urban core no doubt holds many other valuable historical and archaeological secrets that await discovery.

Finding those secrets is going to be difficult, especially if our approach is always one of reaction to development threats. A city of Toronto's size and importance should be led by a comprehensive archaeological master plan that identifies the various sections of the city that have potential for the presence of both precontact aboriginal and post-contact archaeological resources, and which provides clear guidelines about when and where to dig. Many other Ontario municipalities, both large and small, have such plans, including Halton, Waterloo, London, Ottawa-Carleton, Niagara-on-the-Lake, Richmond Hill, Vaughan, and Kingston. In Toronto, small steps are being taken. Recent plans for ambitious waterfront development led to the undertaking of just such a plan for the waterfront area.

The discovery of the archaeological remains of the first Parliament buildings focused the attention of a city and province on a cornerstone of our nation's history, and we have been reminded of why there is a road called Parliament Street leading to our former waterfront. The project has stimulated new and important historical research as well as reflection on how best to commemorate an important historical place. It is also hoped that the project has engendered a new measure of co-operation regarding heritage conservation and interpretation among our various levels of government that in this case, will result in the public's re-discovery of their first "Palaces of Government."

REFERENCES

Archaeological Services Inc.
  1989   *The Historical Documentation of 271 Front Street East, City of Toronto, Ontario.* Ms. on file, Heritage Toronto, Toronto.
  2001   *Report of the Archaeological Assessment of Upper Canada's First and Second Parliament Buildings 1797–1824 and Subsequent Land Uses 1824–2000, 265–271 Front Street East and 25 Berkeley Street, City of Toronto.* Report on file, Culture Division, City of Toronto and Ontario Ministry of Tourism, Culture and Recreation, Toronto.
Arthur, E.
  1979   *From Front Street to Queen's Park.* McClelland and Stewart Limited, Toronto.
  1986   *Toronto: No Mean City* (revised by S.A. Otto). University of Toronto Press, Toronto.
Benn, C.
  1993   *Historic Fort York, 1793–1993.* Natural Heritage/Natural History Inc., Toronto.
  1995   The blockhouses of Toronto: a material history study. *Material History Review* 42.
  1998   A Georgian parish, 1797–1839. In *The Parish and Cathedral of St. James, Toronto 1797–1997,* edited by W. Cooke, pp. 1–37. University of Toronto Press, Toronto.
Bonnycastle, R.H., Sir
  1833   *Plan of the Town and Harbour of York, Upper Canada, and also of the Military Reserve showing the site of the new Barracks and Work around them, as proposed to be erected near the Western Battery.* Royal Engineer Office, U. Canada (signed) R.H. Bonnycastle Captn Royl Engrs Senr Off. Western Districts U.C. 1833; E.T. Ford Lt Royal Engineers ... 1833, Royal Engineers Office Quebec 24th Dec. 1833 [Sgd] Gusts Nicolls Colonel Comg R. Engineer Canada. Ontario Archives, Toronto.
Boulton, W.S., and H.C. Boulton
  1858   *Atlas of Toronto.* Jno Ellis, Toronto.
Browne, J.O., and H.J. Browne
  1862   *Plan of the city of Toronto showing the government survey and the registered subdivision into lots.* Fuller & Bencke, Toronto.
Canada Papers
  1793–1834 Various documents. Chicago Historical Society Archives, Chicago.
City of Toronto Directories
  1964–1999 Various titles, publishers. Toronto Reference Library, Toronto.
Chewett, J.G.
  1830   *A Plan Showing the Survey of part of the park east of the TOWN of YORK, into 1/2 Acre Lots, by Command of His Excellency Sir John Colborne Lieutenant Governor etc., etc., etc. By James G. Chewett, Surveyor, York June 21st 1830.* Microfiche 394 File H-26. Ontario Survey Records, Peterborough.
Consumers' Gas Company
  1887–1940 *Annual Report.* Consumers' Gas Company, Toronto.
  1954   *Blue Flame* 15(5):7.

References

Council of the Corporation of the United Counties of York and Peel
1864–1868 *Report of Standing Committee on County Property and Gaol Management.* Ontario Archives, Toronto.
1869–70 *Commissioners of County Property.* Ontario Archives, Toronto.

Cross, W.K. (editor)
1990 *The Charleton Standard Catalogue of Canadian Colonial Tokens.* 2nd ed. The Charleton Press, Toronto.

Dale, C.A.
1993 *The Palaces of Government: A History of the Legislative Buildings of the Province of Upper Canada and Ontario, 1792–1992.* Microfiche 390 File H–26, Ontario Survey Records. Ontario Legislative Library, Toronto.

Ferris, N.
1986 Buttons I have known. In *Studies in Southwestern Ontario Archaeology,* edited by W.A. Fox, pp. 98–107. Occasional Publications 1. London Chapter of the Ontario Archaeological Society Inc., London.

Firth, E.G. (editor)
1962 *The Town of York 1793–1815: A Collection of Documents of Early Toronto.* The Champlain Society, University of Toronto Press, Toronto.
1966 *The Town of York 1815–1834: A Further Collection of Documents of Early Toronto.* The Champlain Society, University of Toronto Press, Toronto.

Goad, C.E.
1884 *Atlas of the City of Toronto and Suburbs.* C. Goad, Montreal.
1899 *Goad's Atlas of the City of Toronto and Suburbs.* C. Goad, Toronto.
1910 *Goad's Atlas of the City of Toronto and Suburbs.* 3d ed. Wilson and Bunnell, Toronto.

Gurcke, K.
1987 *Bricks and Brickmaking; A Handbook for Historical Archaeology.* University of Idaho Press, Moscow, Idaho.

Hitsman, J.M.
1965 *The Incredible War of 1812: A Military History.* University of Toronto Press, Toronto.

Home District Quarter Session Minutes
1837–1841 MS 251, Reel 2. Ontario Archives, Toronto.

Jones, J.E.
1924 *Pioneer Crimes and Punishments in Toronto and the Home District.* George N. Morang, Toronto.

Journal of the Commons House of Assembly
1798 *Journal of the Commons House of Assembly, Second Session of the Second Parliament.* 3–635 C.O. 42, V. 323. Ontario Archives, Toronto.

Jurney, D.H.
1978 *The Ridge House Cellars: Using Faunal Analysis to Reconstruct Meat Diet.* Unpublished MA thesis, Department of Anthropology, University of Arkansas.

Kenyon, I.
1980 Nineteenth century notes: window glass thickness. *Kewa* 80(2).

Kenyon, T.
1982a Nineteenth century notes: plain T.D. tobacco pipes, part I. *Kewa* 82(3).
1982b Nineteenth century notes: plain T.D. tobacco pipes, part II. *Kewa* 82(4).

1982c   Nineteenth century notes: the 4–band fluted pipe. *Kewa* 80(9).

Kingsford, W.

1855   *Plan of a right of way for the Grand Trunk Railway in front of the City of Toronto, 13 November 1855.* RG 22, Accession 14065, GTR Roll 38. Ontario Archives, Toronto.

Lavallee, O.

1972   *Narrow Gauge Railways of Canada.* Railfare, Montreal.

LeeDecker, C.H., T.H. Klein, C.A. Holt, and A. Friedlander

1987   Nineteenth–century households and consumer behavior in Wilmington, Delaware. In *Consumer Choice in Historical Archaeology*, edited by S.M. Spencer-Wood, pp. 233–259. Plenum Press, New York.

McKee, H.J.

1973   *Introduction to Early American Masonry: Stone, Brick, Mortar and Plaster.* The Preservation Press, Columbia University.

Middleton, J.E.

1934   *Toronto's 100 Years.* City of Toronto, Centennial Publication Committee, Toronto.

Miller, G.L.

1989   *A Chronology of English Shell Edged Pearl and White Wares.* Ms on file, Archaeological Services Inc., Toronto.

Morriss, S.G. (editor)

1982a   *The Journal of John George Howard 1833–49. Book 1 – Volume 1–2 1833–39.* The Ontario Heritage Foundation, Toronto.

1982b   *The Journal of John George Howard 1833–49. Book 2 – Volume 3–4 1840–44.* The Ontario Heritage Foundation, Toronto.

Newlands, D.L.

1979   *Early Ontario Potters: Their Craft and Trade.* McGraw–Hill Ryerson Limited, Toronto.

Nicolls, G.

1816   *Plan of the Harbour, Fort, and Town of York the Capital of Upper Canada, March 16th, 1816.* Dept. of Public Works (197–?), Toronto.

Oliver, P.

1998   *Terror to Evil-doers: Prisons and Punishments in Nineteenth–Century Ontario.* University of Toronto, Toronto.

Otto, S.A.

1993   *Robert Irvine's Movements.* Personal papers of S. Otto.

Papers of Executive Council of Upper Canada

1799   *William Graham: An Estimate of materials and workmanship for to Build a Bl & Guard House ... as per Plan at York, Upper Canada, Febry 16, 1799.* RG 1, E3, Vol. 23/12–13. National Archives, Ottawa.

1806   *The Government of Upper Canada to William Smith: To furnishing Materials and Building a platform and Covered Way between the two Government Buildings ... .* RG 1, E15 B, Vol. 16. National Archives, Ottawa.

1808   *The Government of Upper Canada to John McBeath: To furnishing materials, putting in new sleepers, and laying a new floor in one of the Government Buildings at York ... .* RG 1, E15 B, Vol. 20/7. National Archives, Ottawa.

References

Richardson, A.J.H. and S.A. Otto
1993   The Thomson family: early builders in Upper Canada. *Scarborough Historical Notes and Comments* XVI:4–9.

Scadding, H.
1966   *Toronto of Old*. Edited by F.H. Armstrong. Oxford University Press, Toronto.

Smith, D.W.
1805   *A Sketch showing the Land occupied by John Small Esqre upon the Reserve, appropriated for the Govt House at York, by his Excellency Lt Govr Simcoe.* F/440 Toronto 1805. National Archives, Ottawa.

Smith, S.
1819   *Town of York, April 1819.* D/440 Toronto 1819. National Archives, Ottawa.

Spittal, D.
1996   *Fort York Archaeology Project 1995, Report on Construction Monitoring, Blockhouse No. 2, Building Restoration, Perimeter Drain, Air Conditioning Vault Construction.* Ms on file, Ontario Ministry of Tourism, Culture, and Recreation, Toronto.

Stacey, C.P.
1963   *The Battle of Little York.* Toronto Historical Board, Toronto.

Stewart, E.G.
1958   *Town Gas: Its Manufacture and Distribution.* Science Museum, London.

Sussman, L.
1977   Changes in pearlware dinnerware, 1780–1830. *Historical Archaeology* 11:105–111.
1978   British military tableware, 1760–1830. *Historical Archaeology* 12:93–104.
1997   *Mocha, Banded, Cat's Eye, and Other Factory–Made Slipware.* Studies in Northeast Historical Archaeology Number 1. Boston University, Boston.

Talbot, C.K.
1983   *Justice in Early Ontario, 1791–1840.* Crimecare, Inc., Ottawa.

The Citizens for the Old Town
n.d.   *Old Town 1793: You Can Often See the Vision of a City by How It Views Its Past.* The Citizens for the Old Town & SEDERI, Toronto.

Thomas, S.C.
1987   *Zooarchaeological Analysis of the Lampman Site (AhGx–96), a Nineteenth Century Farm Site near Hamilton, Ontario.* Ms on file, Archaeological Services Inc., Toronto.

Thomson, D.
1797   *David Thomson's Account Book.* On file, Scarborough Historical Society, Toronto.

Tucker, E.
1948   *First Century of Consumers' Gas.* Consumers' Gas Company of Toronto, Toronto.

Turner, W.
1990   *The War of 1812: The War That Both Sides Won.* Dundurn Press, Toronto.

Underwriters Survey Bureau
1954   *Fire Insurance Plans for Toronto.* Plates 9, 10, 19, scale 100 feet: one inch. Ottawa.

Upper Canada State Papers
1819   *Builder's estimate to repair existing brick ruins and build centre building.* RG 1, E3, v.99, p. 84. National Archives, Ottawa.
1830   *Executive Council Report recommending sale of materials from old Parliament Buildings.* RG 1, E3, v.63, pp. 98–99. National Archives, Ottawa.

Upper Canada Sundries

1805   *Proposal to make platforms and covered way between the two Government buildings at York ... .* RG 5, A1, v.4, p. 1511. National Archives, Ottawa.

1806   *Estimate by John McBeath for repairs to the House of Assembly.* RG 5, A1, v.5 pt. 2, p. 2219. National Archives, Ottawa.

1818   *Receipt for stores from No. 1 Brick Building at the lower end of town.* RG 5, A1 v.38. National Archives, Ottawa.

1819   *Thos Ridout Esquire, Proposals ... for erecting Public Buildings at York.* RG 5, A1, p. 110. National Archives, Ottawa.

1826   *2 December 1826 letter from Samuel Chearnley to Sir Peregrine Maitland.* RG 5, A1, p. 43368–70. National Archives, Ottawa.

1828   *1 January 1828 letter from Samuel Chearnley to Major Hillier.* RG 5, A1, p. 47596–9. National Archives, Ottawa.

Warrington, C.J.S. and R.V.V. Nicholls

1949   *A History of Chemistry in Canada.* Pitman and Sons, Toronto.

West, B.

1967   *Toronto.* Doubleday Canada Limited, Toronto.

Westgate, J.H., and P. H. von Bitter

1999   The physical setting: a story of changing environments through time. In *Special Places. The Changing Ecosystems of the Toronto Region*, edited by B.I. Roots, D.A. Chant and C.E. Heidenreich, pp. 10–31. University of British Columbia Press, Vancouver.

Williams, G.

1813   *A Sketch of the Ground at York, Nov. 1813.* NMC-22819. National Archives, Ottawa.

Wilmot, S.

1810   *A Plan Showing the Survey of the land Reserved for the Government Buildings, East end of the Town of York, Surveyed by order of his Excellency Francis Gore Esquire, Lieutenant Governor etc., etc., etc. Drawing date the 18th day of Decr 1810.* Microfiche 390 File H-26. Ontario Survey Records, Peterborough.

INDEX

Note: Page numbers in *italics* refer to illustrations.

Index